SELECTED POEMS

SELECTED POEMS

EDITED BY LOUIS L. MARTZ

A NEW DIRECTIONS BOOK

This selection of poems is based on the following works by H.D.: *Collected
Poems 1912-1944* (1983); *Helen in Egypt* (1961); and *Hermetic Definition*
(1972).

Grateful acknowledgment is given to New Directions Publishing Corp. for
permission to quote from "Canto 83" of *The Cantos of Ezra Pound*
(Copyright 1948 by Ezra Pound).

Manufactured in the United States of America
New Directions Books are printed on acid-free paper; cloth bound editions
are Smyth sewn.
First published clothbound and as New Directions Paperbook 658 in 1988
Published simultaneously in Canada by Penguin Books Canada Limited

Library of Congress Cataloging-in-Publication Data

H. D. (Hilda Doolittle), 1886–1961.
  Selected poems.
  (A New Directions Book)
  I. Martz, Louis Lohr. II. Title.
PS3507.0726A6 1988   811'.52   88-1460
ISBN 0-8112-1065-0
ISBN 0-8112-1066-9 (pbk.)

New Directions Books are published for James Laughlin
by New Directions Publishing Corporation,
80 Eighth Avenue, New York 10011

TABLE OF CONTENTS

INTRODUCTION

I

H.D. is the last of the great generation born in the 1880s to receive due recognition. Pound, Joyce, Eliot, Lawrence, all received early acclaim—notoriety at least, if not their just due; Marianne Moore developed a small but loyal following; and William Carlos Williams, after a long wait, now would find his poetry admired in the circles of the young in terms that equal the acclaim won long ago by his bitterly resented rival Eliot. Why has H.D. lagged behind?

It is not simply because after the appearance of her first volume she became fixed, delimited, by the label *Imagiste* that Pound gave her in 1912, when he sent her early poems to Harriet Monroe for publication in *Poetry*. Pound, of course, never meant to trap her in this way; two years later he was publishing her famous "Oread" in the first issue of *Blast* as an example of "Vorticist" poetry. And indeed "H.D. Vorticist" would have been a better description of her early poetry, with its swirling, dynamic power: the sort of turbulent force that Gaudier-Brzeska described in his own sculptural definition of "Vortex": "Plastic Soul is intensity of life bursting the plane." Or better still, these early poems fit Pound's description of the "image" as "a radiant node or cluster . . . a VORTEX, from which, and through which, and into which, ideas are constantly rushing."[1] This restless movement, the constant surging of intense vitality, lies at the center of H.D.'s early poetry, and thus the static, lapidary, crystalline implications usually carried by the word *imagism* could never contain the strength of H.D.'s muse.

Why, then, did the term cling to her poetry? Partly because H.D. continued to support the movement after Pound had given it over to Amy Lowell and "Amygism"; partly too because the critical and poetical currents of the 1920s and 1930s, under the influence of Eliot and Pound and T.E. Hulme, were violently reacting against romanticism and were insisting upon the need for terse, compact poetry, rich in imagistic inference but spare in abstraction and exclamation. Thus the concentrated imagery of poems such as "Pear Tree" or "Sea Rose" seemed to represent her essence, and her passionate protest against the "Sheltered Garden" could be overlooked.

At the same time H.D. herself contributed to her delimitation and neglect by not publishing, or not collecting, her longer, more powerful, more personal poems, the sequences that showed, as Pound said in a famous footnote, that a "long vorticist poem" was indeed possible.[2] "Amaranth," "Eros," and "Envy," written in Dorset in 1916, out of her anguish at the infidelity of her husband, Richard Aldington, remained unpublished in their original form until 1968. In 1924 H.D. included cut-down versions of these poems under the guise of expansions of fragments from Sappho[3]; these and other poems with Sapphic titles accord with a change in her style of life, and express the problems of that change; but they served to confine her achievement by stressing her role as a translator or adapter of Grecian themes. The powerful assertion of her female identity in "Eurydice" (directed perhaps at D.H. Lawrence)[4] was published in *The Egoist* in 1917—hardly a year for widespread recognition of a poem—but she did not include it in a volume until 1925, too late to remedy the fixation, "Imagiste," in the public eye. And finally, some of the larger poems written during the 1930s, and now coming to be most admired, such as "The Dancer," "The Master," and "The Poet," were either not published at all or appeared only in magazines.

But a deeper reason for the late coming of her reputation underlies all these lesser hindrances. Her basic theme, her basic message to the world, could not be appreciated, indeed, could hardly be heard, until the present time of woman's struggle for liberation and equality. For this is the essential struggle that lies deep within her poetry.

On the flyleaf of the bound typescript that preserves "Amaranth," "Eros," and "Envy," H.D. has written: "from poems of *The Islands* series." We have her poem "The Islands," published in January, 1920, just before her restorative trip to Greece with Winifred Ellerman (Bryher): it is the poem of a deserted woman, an Ariadne on Naxos:

> What are the islands to me
> if you are lost,
> what is Paros to me
> if your eyes draw back,
> what is Milos
> if you take fright of beauty,
> terrible, torturous, isolated,
> a barren rock?

>   *   *   *

> ˌwhat is Greece if you draw back
> from the terror
> and cold splendour of song
> and its bleak sacrifice?

Another poem that seems to belong to this series (which might be labeled "Poems of Desertion and Despair") may be "Toward the Piraeus," published in 1924. The title suggests a poem written as the poet is moving toward the port of Athens and thinking of the disaster dealt with in the "Amaranth" triad. In any case the poem forms a sequel to this triad, a poem in which the poet finds the strength to open by denouncing men, to continue by recognizing the grave flaws in her lover, and to conclude by perceiving that the deeper cause of the disaster lay in her own nature, which had to guard her own sexual and poetical qualities against the pressures of the male, in this case, a faithless soldier-husband and a fellow-poet:

> It was not chastity that made me wild, but fear
> that my weapon, tempered in different heat,
> was over-matched by yours, and your hand
> skilled to yield death-blows, might break

> With the slightest turn—no ill will meant—
> my own lesser, yèt still somewhat fine-wrought,
> fiery-tempered, delicate, over-passionate steel.

It is a good self-assessment, a realization of the vulnerable fragility of her passionate strength.

It was a strength that had within it a frightening intensity: frightening to the self, and to the man concerned, as she has implied in the passages just cited from "The Islands." It is a quality that she presents with terrifying intensity through the cries of "Cassandra," praying to the god Hymen to be relieved of her burden of prophecy, begging to be wed, like other women:

> O Hymen king,
> lord, greatest, power, might,
> look for my face is dark,
> burnt with your light,
> your fire, O Hymen lord;
> is there none left
> can equal me
> in ecstasy, desire?
> is there none left
> can bear with me
> the kiss of your white fire?
> is there not one,
> Phrygian or frenzied Greek,
> poet, song-swept, or bard,
> one meet to take from me
> this bitter power of song,
> one fit to speak, Hymen,
> your praises, lord?
>
> May I not wed
> as you have wed?

H.D. presents this aspect of her nature and her poetry in a splendid passage of the novel *HERmione* (*HER*), where the heroine is talking in the woods with George Lowndes, a figure clearly based on Ezra Pound. Although George calls her a tree-nymph, a "hamadryad," she feels "George could never love a tree properly. . . . George doesn't know what trees are. . . . George doesn't know what I am."[5] The differences that lead to this conclusion are dramatized in the woodland scene where the heroine challenges George to catch her, as she is about to run down a path described in images that mingle the green of trees with the swirling green of water:

> Her own thought, swifter than the thought of George, was there beyond him. "You'll never, never catch me." Her faced George with that, standing on the narrowest of woodpaths that twisted (she knew) a narrow trickle of earth-colour across the green and green that was the steady running of swift water, the steady sweeping and seeping and swirling of branches all about her. If George would catch her, then George would be, might yet be something. (p. 70)

George declines the challenge, saying, "It's too hot, Hermione." But the heat, one supposes, is not so much the weather as the intensity of the girl challenging him; her vitality is more than he can meet, and he declines the match. Hermione then takes off in a turbulent mixture of wood and water images reminiscent of "Oread":

> Heat seeped up, swept down, swirled about them with the green of branches that was torrid tropic water. Green torrid tropic water where no snow fell, where no hint of cold running streams from high mountains swept down, was swept into and under branches that made curious circle and half circle and whole circle. . . . Tree on tree on tree. TREE. I am the Tree of Life. Tree. I am a tree planted by the rivers of water. I am . . . I am . . . HER exactly.

And as those biblical echoes give a transcendent tone to the scene, "Her caught Her to herself, swirled dynamically on flat heels and was off down the trickle of earth-colour that was the path cutting earth-colour through green pellucid water." (p. 70)

What the heroine of H.D.'s novel is discovering in the pervasive earth, wood, and water imagery is the force of her natural love for all created beings: tree or flower, wave or meadow, man or woman. Her creative powers depend upon her ability to enter into the nature of other beings, other creatures, and to feel all the world about her endowed with powers that have no earthly origin. "I am the Tree of Life." The seed of that discovery is planted on the novel's third page:

> The woods parted to show a space of lawn, running level with branches that, in early summer, were white with flower. Dogwood blossom. Pennsylvania. Names are in people, people are in names. Sylvania. I was born here. People ought to think before they call a place Sylvania.
>
> Pennsylvania. I am part of Sylvania. Trees. Trees. Trees. Dogwood, liriodendron with its green-yellow tulip blossoms. Trees are in people. People are in trees. Pennsylvania.

Pound knew something of this. People ought to think before they call a person Dryad. Pound thought, and in the prison camp he found (in Canto 83) the power of that name, as he had felt it in the early poems of "Hilda's Book"—the pamphlet of his love-poems that Ezra bound up and gave to Hilda in their Philadelphia days: "She hath some tree-born spirit of the wood / About her, and the wind is in her hair." ("Rendez-vous")[6] In the context of "Hilda's Book" and the tree-imagery of *HERmione*, Pound's poem "The Tree" may be read as an appeal for mutual understanding, a declaration that the male speaker shares something of his Dryad's mysterious source of knowledge and power. It is about the mystery of metamorphic union in love: Daphne transmuted into the laurel that crowns her lover Apollo and all poets, or Baucis and Philemon, united as two trees. Such mysteries of transformation cannot be performed without the power of mutual love:

'Twas not until the gods had been

Kindly entreated and been brought within
Unto the hearth of their hearts' home
That they might do this wonder thing.
Naethless I have been a tree amid the wood
And many new things understood
That were rank folly to my head before.

Of course he could not truly understand her, nor could Aldington, nor could Lawrence, nor could Cecil Gray—though Lawrence, being close to her in his response to life, might have come to understand her, if Frieda had not been on guard. H.D. was left alone.

II

Although the poems of "The Islands" series often seem despairing, their center is strong and it does not give way. The voice of Eurydice, after denouncing the ruthlessness and arrogance of her lover, retains the integrity of her self:

At least I have the flowers of myself,
and my thoughts, no god
can take that;
I have the fervour of myself for a presence
and my own spirit for light . . .

Such an attitude leads on to the major poems, some apparently and some certainly composed in the 1930s, especially the powerful triad, "The Dancer," "The Master," and "The Poet," composed after her treatment by Freud in 1933 and 1934. "The Dancer," perhaps in part evoking memories of Isadora Duncan's Greek and erotic modes of dancing, is her supreme assertion of woman's integrity as artist and sexual force (the two are for H.D., as for Lawrence and Duncan, inseparable). This poem leads directly into "The Master," a tribute to Freud much franker than her prose tribute, for it deals openly with her bi-sexuality ("I had two loves separate") and also shows her disagreement with Freud's diagnosis of her need for a male to sustain her. But she is grateful, deeply grateful, to Freud for his confidence in her creative gift: "you are a poet," "you are a poet"—she repeats his words, as a sign of the reassurance that he gave her, and a sign of how, as she says, "it was he himself, he who set me free / to prophesy." Free from self-doubt—to prophesy— what? To prophesy the freedom of woman from bondage to the male, but not alienation from the male, as her moving tribute to "The Poet" shows in the third poem of this triptych. The poet concerned is, almost certainly, Law- rence, as the allusion to the "small coptic temple" indicates with its apparent reference to the "shrine" on the mountain above Taos.

The delicate balance of attitudes displayed in this triad has not been easily achieved, as we may see from the long poem "Calypso" (or "Callypso", to use H.D.'s spelling), known since 1938 from its brief second part, which H.D. published in *Poetry* under the caption "From Episode I." This part, by itself, creates a sharp, ironical contrast be- tween Calypso's bitter denunciation of Odysseus as a forget- ful brute, and the attitude revealed by his own speech, where he is sensitively remembering her generous favors. As published complete in 1983, the whole of "Calypso" pre- sents a highly complex dialogue, or set of monologues, on the invasion of female privacy and peace by the male force. Literally, at the outset, Calypso is speaking as she watches Odysseus land and climb up the cliff, but the sudden shift at the close of this part, along with the strong sexual images throughout, make it plain that what we are watching is the sexual encounter itself, resisted by the female, forced by the male, and ending with both at peace, the male asleep with the woman's "hair spread on his chest," and the woman saying "he shall never get away." The whole poem repre- sents a complex weaving of sexual themes: resistance, vio- lence, peace, possessiveness, severance, anger, sadness.

Both man and woman have combined to create the saving of the gift for H.D. Bryher saved her in 1919 when, after the birth of her daughter, the deaths of her brother and father, and the breaking with Aldington and Lawrence, she is near death, both physically and mentally. Her tribute to Bryher appears in the sequence "Let Zeus Record," pub- lished in *Red Roses for Bronze* (1931); it speaks, with love and admiration, of a relationship that is ending. *Red Roses for Bronze* concludes with both an "Epitaph" and a "Renaissance Choros" ("The Mysteries")—"Renaissance" suggesting both a new era of culture and a time for personal rebirth under the power of the religious faith and figure represented in the "voice" that speaks out of the dark turbulence of the opening section: "peace / be still"—the words of Christ (Mark 4:39) that calm the storm at sea. The poem continues with allusions to the Gospels, especially to the parables, combining these with allusions to the pagan mystery cults as the "voice" concludes:

"The mysteries remain,
I keep the same
cycle of seed-time
and of sun and rain;
Demeter in the grass
I multiply,
renew and bless
Iacchus in the vine. . . .

*I keep the law,
I hold the mysteries true,
I am the vine,
the branches, you
and you.*"

This concluding poem of 1931 is closely linked, both in style and in subject, with the poem "The Magician" (Christ is called a "magician" in the second section of "The Mysteries"), published in an obscure magazine in January, 1933, two months before H.D. began her treatments with Freud. This poem is spoken in the person of a disciple of Christ who has heard his words and witnessed his miracles, and who now places reliance, not upon the symbols of the Crucifixion, but upon the images of nature that appear in the parables: nature as a channel toward the divine. Both the ending of *Red Roses for Bronze* and "The Magician" show that H.D. had not utterly lost her creative powers when she sought help from Freud. She was capable of writing well, and Freud seems to have realized that her condition did not require the sort of deep analysis that would occupy years. A few months of advice would, and did, suffice to bring forth an immense surge of creative power, represented in "The Dancer" triad and in the completion of her long-contemplated version of the *Ion* of Euripides, published in 1937.

H.D. had more to prophesy than female equality: she felt in the thirties what she had felt during World War I, the need of redemption for a whole society, as expressed in her long sequence of 1916, "The Tribute," a poem that shows H.D.'s acute sensitivity to contemporary events. So too now in the middle thirties, her version of the *Ion*, with its interspersed prose commentary, urges the distressed world not to despair: as the *Ion* represents the birth of Greek (Ionian) culture, so now, a new era may yet be born for Europe. Thus H.D. carries on the dual message of all prophets: her eye is on the problems of the present, whose evils she can firmly denounce, yet her prophecies offer hope and consolation, after the manner of the Hebrew prophets, who mingled denunciations of doom with promises of salvation. In this redemption the liberated role of woman was to play an indispensable part.

So now the way is ready for H.D. to write her wartime *Trilogy*, completed in December of 1944, poems inspired by her living in London throughout the worst years of the bombing. The work is sometimes called epic, but, like the later *Helen in Egypt*, it seems rather to belong to the genre of prophecy, because it consists of a sequence of short lyric or meditative utterances, presenting a series of inner voices and visions amid the ruins of London:

> ruin everywhere, yet as the fallen roof
> leaves the sealed room
> open to the air,
>
> so, through our desolation,
> thoughts stir, inspiration stalks us
> through gloom:

unaware, Spirit announces the Presence . . .

And soon she hears a Voice speaking above the "whirr and roar in the high air," and she has her strange vision of the Egyptian gods, Ra, Osiris, Amen-Ra, appearing "in a spacious, bare meeting-house" such as she knew in Philadelphia or in her Moravian childhood, in Bethlehem, Pennsylvania. All religions for her, as for Lawrence in his later writings, are blending into one; the goal is to:

> recover the secret of Isis,
> which is: there was One
>
> in the beginning, Creator,
> Fosterer, Begetter, the Same-forever
>
> in the papyrus-swamp
> in the Judean meadow.

Here the technique of parallelism and repetition, in the distich form, is reminiscent of biblical poetry: it is a technique followed throughout *Trilogy*, except for the prologue in tercets.

The first part of the trilogy, *The Walls Do Not Fall*, is preparatory, exploratory, an assertion of belief. The finding of the secret of Isis comes in the second part, *Tribute to the Angels*, which begins under the guidance of the mythical Hermes Trismegistus, father of language and founder of ancient Egyptian culture: but his influence merges with the book of Revelation and the Gospels as H.D. recalls how the author of the book of Revelation had tried to warn off future prophets by saying at the end, "If any man shall add unto these things, God shall add unto him the plagues that are written in this book." H.D. remembers this, but she also remembers that the figure of Christ in the prophecy itself had said something quite different:

> *I John saw. I testify;*
> *if any man shall add*

God shall add unto him the plagues,
but he that sat upon the throne said,

I make all things new.
I John saw. I testify,

but *I make all things new,*
said He of the seven stars . . .

Here she recalls what Christ said from the throne in
Chapter 21 of the book of Revelation: "Behold, I make all
things new. And he said unto me, Write: for these words are
true and faithful." And so, with this word, she writes and
discovers soon the very sign of renewal as springtime in
London brings forth flowers and new shoots of trees among
the ruins (like the charred olive-tree of Athene that her
devotee finds on the ruined Acropolis):[7]

the lane is empty but the levelled wall

is purple as with purple spread
upon an altar,

this is the flowering of the rood,
this is the flowering of the reed . . .

Then she walks through a ruined wall and sees:

a half-burnt-out apple-tree
blossoming;

this is the flowering of the rood,
this is the flowering of the wood,

where Annael, we pause to give
thanks that we rise again from death and live.

From here she moves on to a dream-vision such as
Freud had taught her to trust, the dream of a Lady in White.
Was it the Virgin Mary? She teases us with this idea for a

while, recalling the Madonnas of the painters, but no, the Lady could not be this, because "she bore / none of her usual attributes; / the Child was not with her." Who then was she?

> Ah (you say), this is Holy Wisdom,
> Santa Sophia, the SS of the Sanctus Spiritus,
>
> so by facile reasoning, logically
> the incarnate symbol of the Holy Ghost . . .

H.D. is teasing here the academic reader given to such learned interpretations:

> O yes—you understand, I say,
> this is all most satisfactory,
>
> but she wasn't hieratic, she wasn't frozen,
> she wasn't very tall . . .
>
> she carries a book but it is not
> the tome of the ancient wisdom,
>
> the pages, I imagine, are the blank pages
> of the unwritten volume of the new;
>
> all you say, is implicit,
> all that and much more . . .
>
> she is Psyche, the butterfly,
> out of the cocoon.

She is the prophetic spirit of the poet, released now to relate in the third part of her trilogy, *The Flowering of the Rod*, a relaxed and happy fable of redemption that tells how Mary Magdalen obtained from Kaspar, one of the Magi, the jar from which she anointed the feet of Christ. It is a tale of healing addressed not only to London but to all the "smouldering cities" of Europe, as the opening sections here included make clear.

Her use of the myth of Isis in the *Trilogy* leads on to the central image of her longest and most difficult poem, *Helen in Egypt*, published in the year of her death, 1961, but completed in 1952–55. It is a work of intermingled prose and poetry, like the *Ion*. After the poetical sequence was completed in 1954, H.D. composed what she called "captions" to go with each poem, and she directed their placement. So there the captions are, and their presence creates a different work from the purely poetical sequence that she originally composed. (In this selection some of the longer captions have been omitted.) We may prefer to read the poems by themselves, but we can hardly ignore the captions entirely. The question is: How do they function?

We may find an answer by remembering how often the prophetic writings of the Bible, as in the books of Isaiah or Jeremiah, intermingle poetry and prose, with the effect that the prose creates a setting, or an explanation, for the poem that follows. In this analogy lies perhaps a key to the *kind* of work she is writing, and thus a key to the way in which we might deal with her intermingling of poetry and prose, here as well as in the *Ion*. If we regard *Helen in Egypt* as belonging to the genre of prophecy, we can perhaps see more clearly how the various voices in the poem work— including the prose voices. As the example of the Hebrew prophets will indicate, it is the role of the prophet to hear voices and to speak forth the words of those voices. The very word *prophet*, in Greek, means "one who speaks for another"—for God, for the gods, or for other human beings.

From the opening poems in *Helen in Egypt*, H.D.'s Helen speaks with the voice of a prophet, saying "in this Amen-temple" (the temple of Amen-Ra, or Zeus-Ammon, in Egypt) she hears the "voices" of "the hosts / surging beneath the Walls" of Troy, voices that cry

O Helen, Helen, Daemon that thou art,

we will be done forever
with this charm, this evil philtre,
this curse of Aphrodite . . .

But the third poem presents a voice of redemption as Helen
says

> Alas, my brothers,
> Helen did not walk
> upon the ramparts,
>
> she whom you cursed
> was but the phantom and the shadow thrown
> of a reflection;
>
> you are forgiven for I know my own,
> and God for his own purpose
> wills it so, that I
>
> stricken, forsaken draw to me,
> through magic greater than the trial of arms,
> your own invincible, unchallenged Sire . . .

The poem is based on the alternate myth of Helen which
Euripides used in his play on that subject and which Richard
Strauss used for his opera *The Egyptian Helen*. Here the
story says that Helen never was in Troy, but that the gods
sent there a phantom of Helen, while the true Helen was
transported by Zeus to Egypt where, after the war, she was
reunited with Menelaus, or in H.D.'s version, with Achilles:

> But this Helen is not to be recognized by earthly
> splendour nor this Achilles by accoutrements of
> valour. It is the lost legions that have conditi-
> oned their encounter, and "the sea-enchantment
> in his eyes."
>
> How did we know each other?
> was it the sea-enchantment in his eyes
> of Thetis, his sea-mother?

In that phrase "the sea-enchantment in his eyes" we meet in
both the prose and the poetry the leading phrase and sym-
bol of the work, for Thetis will, as the sequence proceeds, be

merged with Aphrodite, also born of the sea, and with Isis, called in the prose "the Egyptian Aphrodite." Helen herself is in the latter part of the work transformed into a living symbol of all these goddesses: the love of Achilles for Helen, then, suggests a way of redeeming the war-torn world, as the voice of Helen has said very early in the poem:

> it was God's plan
> to melt the icy fortress of the soul,
> and free the man . . .

All this is quite in accord with the dual meaning of the work that H.D. has suggested in a letter to Norman Pearson, where she says that her poem has both "exoteric" meaning related to "all war problems . . . as well as being strictly INNER and esoteric and personal."[8] That is to say, the imagery of war suggests the problems raised by war for all mankind down through the ages, along with the personal problems that such wars cause for individual lives, and caused, as we know, for H.D. herself, witness of two wars. Helen has taken within herself the sufferings of the whole war-stricken world:

> mine, the great spread of wings,
> the thousand sails,
> the thousand feathered darts
>
> that sped them home,
> mine, the one dart in the Achilles-heel,
> the thousand-and-one, mine.

To say that Helen speaks throughout as the prophet or priestess of Isis would be to sum up the meaning of the work, for Isis is the benevolent, creative goddess of love, known throughout the Mediterranean world as the "Goddess of many names."

The reconciliation that love creates between Helen and Achilles (a figure based upon H.D.'s wartime acquaintance with Sir Hugh Dowding, head of the British Fighter Command) is part of a long process of personal reconciliations.

Though her poems absorb, re-create, and transcend the biographical element, the personal dimension is always there. Her reconciliations include, first, Lawrence, as she makes clear in *Advent*, the diary of her consultations with Freud, in "The Poet" (as it seems), and perhaps also in the latter part of the enigmatic sequence "Sigil," from which poem XI was published in 1931, the year after Lawrence's death.[9] Reconciliation with Aldington was much more difficult, as one may see from her treatment of the wholly destructive figure of Paris in *Helen in Egypt*. Yet acceptance, at least, came at the end, as some lines from "Winter Love" indicate:

> Paris-Oenone?
>
> Helen, commend their happiness
> and so invoke the greater bliss
> of Helios-Helen-Eros.

Reconciliation with Pound is the chief impetus within "Winter Love," and here the reconciliation was easier, since Pound had made amends in the "Dryad" passage of his Pisan Canto 83:

> Δρυάς, your eyes are like clouds
>
> Nor can who has passed a month in the death cells
>   believe in capital punishment
> No man who has passed a month in the death cells
>   believes in cages for beasts
>
> Δρυάς, your eyes are like the clouds over Taishan
>   When some of the rain has fallen
>   and half remains yet to fall . . .
>
>   Dryad, thy peace is like water
> There is September sun on the pools

The passage seems to evoke the memory of the early sonnet to Hilda entitled "PAX" (a word twice used thematically in the earlier part of Canto 83):

> Meseemeth that 'tis sweet this wise to lie
> Somewhile quite parted from the stream of things
> Watching alone the clouds' high wanderings
> As free as they are in some wind-free sky
> While naught but thoughts of thee as clouds glide
>   by . . .

"Winter Love" returns the memory, recalling in section 5 the parental interdiction of their embraces:

> the rough stones of a wall,
> the fragrance of honey-flowers, the bees,
> and how I would have fallen but for a voice,
>
> calling through the brambles
> and tangle of bay-berry
> and rough broom,
>
> *Helen, Helen, come home*;
> there was a Helen before there was a War,
> but who remembers her?

Then section 6 recalls the shock of the lover's departure on his ship.

"Euphorion," the mythic child of Helen and Achilles in *Helen in Egypt,* here becomes, in accord with the Greek root of the word, an allegorical figure of "well-being," a state of health, a state of hope, a symbol of poetry. But the hope ("Espérance") is hard to hold: as death threatens the poet, the "Child" of Helios-Helen-Eros is almost more than the writer can bear. For a time (like Cassandra in her poem) H.D. begs the presiding mother-goddess to relieve her of this prophetic burden, but in the end her strength survives:

> I die in agony whether I give or do not give;
> cruel, cruel *Sage-Femme,*
>
> wiser than all the regents of God's throne,

why do you torture me?
come, come, O *Espérance*,

Espérance, O golden bee,
take life afresh and if you must,
so slay me.

LOUIS L. MARTZ

NOTES

1. Ezra Pound, *Gaudier-Brzeska* (New York: New Directions, 1960), pp. 21, 92.
2. *Gaudier-Brzeska*, p. 94.
3. For detailed discussion of these revisions see *H.D.: Collected Poems, 1912–1944* (New York: New Directions, 1983), pp. xiv–xviii, 617–18.
4. See *H.D.: Collected Poems, 1912–1944*, p. xx.
5. *HERmione* (New York: New Directions, 1984), pp. 73, 84.
6. "Hilda's Book" is published as an appendix to H.D.'s memoir of Pound, *End to Torment*, ed. Norman Holmes Pearson and Michael King (New York: New Directions, 1979). For the close relation between the novel *HER* and "Hilda's Book" see the essay by Susan Friedman in *Poesis* 6 (1985), 56–73.
7. See the passage from H.D.'s *Ion* in this selection, p. 125.
8. See her unpublished letter to Norman Pearson, November 26, 1955, which also contains her directions concerning the "captions." (H.D. Archive, Beinecke Library, Yale University)
9. For the relation of this sequence to *Women in Love* see the essay by Gary Burnett in *H.D. Newsletter* 1 (1987), 32–35.

ACKNOWLEDGMENTS

We wish to express our gratitude to Perdita Schaffner for permission to publish her mother's writings, and to the Beinecke Rare Book and Manuscript Library of Yale University for permission to study and publish materials from the H.D. Archive in that library. The editor wishes to thank Carolyn Grassi for valuable advice and assistance in the preparation of this selection.

SELECTED POEMS

Sea Rose

Rose, harsh rose,
marred and with stint of petals,
meagre flower, thin,
sparse of leaf,

more precious
than a wet rose
single on a stem—
you are caught in the drift.

Stunted, with small leaf,
you are flung on the sand,
you are lifted
in the crisp sand
that drives in the wind.

Can the spice-rose
drip such acrid fragrance
hardened in a leaf?

Sea Lily

Reed,
slashed and torn
but doubly rich—
such great heads as yours
drift upon temple-steps,
but you are shattered
in the wind.

Myrtle-bark
is flecked from you,
scales are dashed
from your stem,
sand cuts your petal,
furrows it with hard edge,
like flint
on a bright stone.

Yet though the whole wind
slash at your bark,
you are lifted up,
aye—though it hiss
to cover you with froth.

Evening

The light passes
from ridge to ridge,
from flower to flower—
the hepaticas, wide-spread
under the light
grow faint—
the petals reach inward,
the blue tips bend
toward the bluer heart
and the flowers are lost.

The cornel-buds are still white,
but shadows dart
from the cornel-roots—
black creeps from root to root,
each leaf
cuts another leaf on the grass,
shadow seeks shadow,
then both leaf
and leaf-shadow are lost.

Sheltered Garden

I have had enough.
I gasp for breath.

Every way ends, every road,
every foot-path leads at last
to the hill-crest—
then you retrace your steps,
or find the same slope on the other side,
precipitate.

I have had enough—
border-pinks, clove-pinks, wax-lilies,
herbs, sweet-cress.

O for some sharp swish of a branch—
there is no scent of resin
in this place,
no taste of bark, of coarse weeds,
aromatic, astringent—
only border on border of scented pinks.

Have you seen fruit under cover
that wanted light—
pears wadded in cloth,
protected from the frost,

melons, almost ripe,
smothered in straw?

Why not let the pears cling
to the empty branch?
All your coaxing will only make
a bitter fruit—
let them cling, ripen of themselves,
test their own worth,
nipped, shrivelled by the frost,
to fall at last but fair
with a russet coat.

Or the melon—
let it bleach yellow
in the winter light,
even tart to the taste—
it is better to taste of frost—
the exquisite frost—
than of wadding and of dead grass.

For this beauty,
beauty without strength,
chokes out life.
I want wind to break,
scatter these pink-stalks,
snap off their spiced heads,
fling them about with dead leaves—
spread the paths with twigs,
limbs broken off,
trail great pine branches,
hurled from some far wood
right across the melon-patch,
break pear and quince—
leave half-trees, torn, twisted
but showing the fight was valiant.

O to blot out this garden
to forget, to find a new beauty
in some terrible
wind-tortured place.

Sea Poppies

Amber husk
fluted with gold,
fruit on the sand
marked with a rich grain,

treasure
spilled near the shrub-pines
to bleach on the boulders:

your stalk has caught root
among wet pebbles
and drift flung by the sea
and grated shells
and split conch-shells.

Beautiful, wide-spread,
fire upon leaf,
what meadow yields
so fragrant a leaf
as your bright leaf?

Garden

I

You are clear
O rose, cut in rock,
hard as the descent of hail.

I could scrape the colour
from the petals
like spilt dye from a rock.

If I could break you
I could break a tree.

If I could stir
I could break a tree—
I could break you.

II

O wind, rend open the heat,
cut apart the heat,
rend it to tatters.

Fruit cannot drop
through this thick air—
fruit cannot fall into heat
that presses up and blunts
the points of pears
and rounds the grapes.

Cut the heat—
plough through it,
turning it on either side
of your path.

Sea Violet

The white violet
is scented on its stalk,
the sea-violet
fragile as agate,
lies fronting all the wind
among the torn shells
on the sand-bank.

The greater blue violets
flutter on the hill,
but who would change for these
who would change for these
one root of the white sort?

Violet
your grasp is frail
on the edge of the sand-hill,
but you catch the light—
frost, a star edges with its fire.

Orchard

I saw the first pear
as it fell—
the honey-seeking, golden-banded,
the yellow swarm
was not more fleet than I,
(spare us from loveliness)
and I fell prostrate
crying:
you have flayed us
with your blossoms,
spare us the beauty
of fruit-trees.

The honey-seeking
paused not,
the air thundered their song,
and I alone was prostrate.

O rough-hewn
god of the orchard,
I bring you an offering—
do you, alone unbeautiful,
son of the god,
spare us from loveliness:

these fallen hazel-nuts,
stripped late of their green sheaths,
grapes, red-purple,
their berries

dripping with wine,
pomegranates already broken,
and shrunken figs
and quinces untouched,
I bring you as offering.

Sea Gods

I

They say there is no hope—
sand—drift—rocks—rubble of the sea—
the broken hulk of a ship,
hung with shreds of rope,
pallid under the cracked pitch.

They say there is no hope
to conjure you—
no whip of the tongue to anger you—
no hate of words
you must rise to refute.

They say you are twisted by the sea,
you are cut apart
by wave-break upon wave-break,
that you are misshapen by the sharp rocks,
broken by the rasp and after-rasp.

That you are cut, torn, mangled,
torn by the stress and beat,
no stronger than the strips of sand
along your ragged beach.

II

But we bring violets,
great masses—single, sweet,

wood-violets, stream-violets,
violets from a wet marsh.

Violets in clumps from hills,
tufts with earth at the roots,
violets tugged from rocks,
blue violets, moss, cliff, river-violets.

Yellow violets' gold,
burnt with a rare tint—
violets like red ash
among tufts of grass.

We bring deep-purple
bird-foot violets.

We bring the hyacinth-violet,
sweet, bare, chill to the touch—
and violets whiter than the in-rush
of your own white surf.

III

For you will come,
you will yet haunt men in ships,
you will trail across the fringe of strait
and circle the jagged rocks.

You will trail across the rocks
and wash them with your salt,
you will curl between sand-hills—
you will thunder along the cliff—
break—retreat—get fresh strength—
gather and pour weight upon the beach.

You will draw back,
and the ripple on the sand-shelf
will be witness of your track.
O privet-white, you will paint
the lintel of wet sand with froth.

You will bring myrrh-bark
and drift laurel-wood from hot coasts!
when you hurl high—high—
we will answer with a shout.

For you will come,
you will come,
you will answer our taut hearts,
you will break the lie of men's thoughts,
and cherish and shelter us.

Storm

You crash over the trees,
you crack the live branch—
the branch is white,
the green crushed,
each leaf is rent like split wood.

You burden the trees
with black drops,
you swirl and crash—
you have broken off a weighted leaf
in the wind,
it is hurled out,
whirls up and sinks,
a green stone.

Sea Iris

I

Weed, moss-weed,
root tangled in sand,

sea-iris, brittle flower,
one petal like a shell
is broken,
and you print a shadow
like a thin twig.

Fortunate one,
scented and stinging,
rigid myrrh-bud,
camphor-flower,
sweet and salt—you are wind
in our nostrils.

II

Do the murex-fishers
drench you as they pass?
Do your roots drag up colour
from the sand?
Have they slipped gold under you—
rivets of gold?

Band of iris-flowers
above the waves,
you are painted blue,
painted like a fresh prow
stained among the salt weeds.

Hermes of the Ways

The hard sand breaks,
and the grains of it
are clear as wine.

Far off over the leagues of it,
the wind,
playing on the wide shore,

piles little ridges,
and the great waves
break over it.

But more than the many-foamed ways
of the sea,
I know him
of the triple path-ways,
Hermes,
who awaits.

Dubious,
facing three ways,
welcoming wayfarers,
he whom the sea-orchard
shelters from the west,
from the east
weathers sea-wind;
fronts the great dunes.

Wind rushes
over the dunes,
and the coarse, salt-crusted grass
answers.

Heu,
it whips round my ankles!

II

Small is
this white stream,
flowing below ground
from the poplar-shaded hill,
but the water is sweet.

Apples on the small trees
are hard,
too small,

too late ripened
by a desperate sun
that struggles through sea-mist.

The boughs of the trees
are twisted
by many bafflings;
twisted are
the small-leafed boughs.

But the shadow of them
is not the shadow of the mast head
nor of the torn sails.

Hermes, Hermes,
the great sea foamed,
gnashed its teeth about me;
but you have waited,
where sea-grass tangles with
shore-grass.

Pear Tree

Silver dust
lifted from the earth,
higher than my arms reach,
you have mounted,
O silver,
higher than my arms reach
you front us with great mass;

no flower ever opened
so staunch a white leaf,
no flower ever parted silver
from such rare silver;

O white pear,
your flower-tufts
thick on the branch
bring summer and ripe fruits
in their purple hearts.

Oread

Whirl up, sea—
whirl your pointed pines,
splash your great pines
on our rocks,
hurl your green over us,
cover us with your pools of fir.

The Pool

Are you alive?
I touch you.
You quiver like a sea-fish.
I cover you with my net.
What are you—banded one?

Moonrise

Will you glimmer on the sea?
will you fling your spear-head
on the shore?
what note shall we pitch?
we have a song,
on the bank we share our arrows;
the loosed string tells our note:

O flight,
bring her swiftly to our song.
She is great,
we measure her by the pine trees.

From The Tribute

1

Squalor spreads its hideous length
through the carts and the asses' feet,
squalor coils and reopens
and creeps under barrow
and heap of refuse
and the broken sherds
of the market-place—
it lengthens and coils
and uncoils and draws back
and recoils
through the crooked streets.

Squalor blights and makes hideous
our lives—it has smothered
the beat of our songs,
and our hearts are spread out,
flowers—opened but to receive
the wheel of the cart,

the hoof of the ox,
to be trod of the sheep.

Squalor spreads its hideous length
through the carts and the asses' feet—
squalor has entered and taken our songs
and we haggle and cheat,
praise fabrics worn threadbare,
ring false coin for silver,
offer refuse for meat.

2

While we shouted our wares
with the swindler and beggar,
our cheap stuffs for the best,
while we cheated and haggled and bettered
each low trick
and railed with the rest—

In a trice squalor failed,
even squalor to cheat
for a voice
caught the sky in one sudden note,
spread grass at the horses' feet,
spread a carpet of scented thyme
and meadow-sweet
till the asses lifted their heads
to the air
with the stifled cattle and sheep.

Ah, squalor was cheated at last
for a bright head flung back,
caught the ash-tree fringe
of the foot-hill,
the violet slope of the hill,
one bright head flung back
stilled the haggling,
one throat bared
and the shouting was still.

Clear, clear—
till our heart's shell was reft
with the shrill notes,
our old hatreds were healed.

Squalor spreads its hideous length
through the carts and the asses' feet,
squalor coils and draws back
and recoils
with no voice to rebuke—
for the boys have gone out of the city,
the songs withered black on their lips.

3

And we turn from the market,
the haggling, the beggar, the cheat,
to cry to the gods of the city
in the open space
of the temple—
we enter the temple-space
to cry to the gods and forget
the clamour, the filth.

We turn to the old gods of the city,
of the city once blessed
with daemon and spirit of blitheness
and spirit of mirth,
we cry;
what god with shy laughter,
or with slender winged ankles is left?

What god, what bright spirit for us,
what daemon is left
of the many that crowded the porches
that haunted the streets,
what fair god
with bright sandal and belt?

Though we tried the old turns of the city
and searched the old streets,
though we cried to the gods of the city:
O spirits, turn back,
re-enter the gates of our city—
we met
but one god,
one tall god with a spear-shaft,
one bright god with a lance.

4

They have sent the old gods from the city:
on the temple step,
the people gather to cry for revenge,
to chant their hymns and to praise
the god of the lance.

They have banished the gods
and the half-gods
from the city streets,
they have turned from the god
of the cross roads,
the god of the hearth,
the god of the sunken well
and the fountain source,
they have chosen one,
to him only
they offer paean and chant.

Though but one god is left in the city,
shall we turn to his treacherous feet,
though but one god is left in the city,
can he lure us
with his clamour and shout,
can he snare our hearts in his net,
can he blind us
with the light of his lance?

Could he snare our spirit and flesh,
he would cast it in irons to lie
and rot in the sodden grass,
and we know his glamour is dross,
we know him a blackened light,
and his beauty withered and spent
beside one young life that is lost.

5

Though not one of the city turned,
not one girl but to glance
with contempt toward us
that our hearts were so faint
with despair and doubt,
contempt for us that our lips
could not sing to the god of the lance—

Though not one of the city turned
as we searched through the city streets,
though the maidens gathered their veils
and the women their robes
as we passed:—

Though not one of the city turned
as we paused at the city gate,
a few old men rose up
with eyes no fear or contempt
could harden—with lips worn frail
with no words of hate.

A few old men rose up
with a few sad women to greet and to hail us,
a few lads crept to welcome
and comfort us, their white brows
set with hope
as light circles an olive-branch.

With these we will cry to another,
with these we will stand apart
to lure some god to our city,
to hail him:
return from your brake,
your copse or your forest haunt.

O spirit still left to our city,
we call to your wooded haunt,
we cry:
O daemon of grasses,
O spirit of simples and roots,
O gods of the plants of the earth—

O god of the simples and grasses,
we cry to you now from our hearts,
O heal us—bring balm for our sickness,
return and soothe us with bark
and hemlock and feverwort.

O god of the power to strike out
memory of terror past,
bring branch of heal-all and tufts,
of the sweet and the bitter grass,
bring shaft and flower of the reeds
and cresses and meadow plants.

Return—look again on our city,
though the people cry through the streets,
though they hail another,
have pity—return to our gates,
with a love as great as theirs,
we entreat you
for our city's sake.

Amaranth

I

Am I blind alas,
am I blind,
I too have followed
her path.
I too have bent at her feet.
I too have wakened to pluck
amaranth in the straight shaft,
amaranth purple in the cup,
scorched at the edge to white.

Am I blind?
am I the less ready for her sacrifice?
am I less eager to give
what she asks,
she the shameless and radiant?

Am I quite lost,
I towering above you and her glance,
walking with swifter pace,
with clearer sight,
with intensity
beside which you two
are as spent ash?

Nay I give back to my goddess the gift
she tendered me in a moment
of great bounty.
I return it. I lay it again
on the white slab of her house,
the beauty she cast out
one moment, careless.

Nor do I cry out:

"why did I stoop?
why did I turn aside
one moment from the rocks
marking the sea-path?
Andromeda, shameless and radiant,
have pity, turn, answer us."

Ah no—though I stumble toward
her altar-step,
though my flesh is scorched and rent,
shattered, cut apart,
and slashed open;
though my heels press my own wet life
black, dark to purple,
on the smooth rose-streaked
threshold of her pavement.

II

Am I blind, alas, deaf too,
that my ears lost all this?
Nay, O my lover, Atthis:
shameless and still radiant
I tell you this:

I was not asleep.
I did not lie asleep on those hot rocks
while you waited.
I was not unaware when I glanced
out toward sea,
watching the purple ships.

I was not blind when I turned.
I was not indifferent when I strayed aside
or loitered as we three went,
or seemed to turn a moment from the path
for that same amaranth.

I was not dull and dead when I fell
back on our couch at night.
I was not indifferent though I turned
and lay quiet.
I was not dead in my sleep.

III

Lady of all beauty,
I give you this:
say I have offered but small sacrifice,
say I am unworthy your touch,
but say not, I turned to some cold, calm god,
silent, pitiful, in preference.

Lady of all beauty,
I give you this:
say not, I have deserted your altar-steps,
that the fire on your white hearth
was too great,
that I fell back at your first glance.

Lady, radiant and shameless,
I have brought small wreaths,
they were a child's gift.
I have offered you white myrrh-leaf
and sweet lentisk.
I have laid rose-petals
and white rock-rose from the beach.

But I give now
a greater,
I give life and spirit with this,
I render a grace
no one has dared to speak
at your carved altar-step,
lest men point him out,
slave, callous to your art,

I dare more than the singer
offering her lute,
the girl her stained veils,
the woman her swathes of birth,
the older woman her pencils of chalk
and mirror and unguent box.

I offer more than the lad,
singing at your steps,
praising himself mirrored in his friend's face,
more than any girl,
I offer you this,
(grant only strength
that I withdraw not my gift)
I give you my praise for this:
the love of my lover for his mistress.

IV

Let him go forth radiant,
let life rise in his young breast,
life is radiant,
life is made for beautiful love
and strange ecstasy,
strait, searing body and limbs,
tearing limbs and body from life;
life is his if he ask,
life is his if he take it,
then let him take beauty
as his right.

Take beauty, wander apart
in the tree-shadows,
wander under wind-bowed sheaths
of golden fir-boughs,
go far, far from here
in your happiness,
take beauty for that is her wish:

Her wish,
the radiant and shameless.

V

But I,
how I hate you for this,
how I despise and hate,
was my beauty so slight a gift,
so soon, so soon forgot?

I hate you for this,
and now that your fault be less,
I would cry, turn back,
lest she the shameless and radiant
slay you for neglect.

Neglect of the finest beauty upon earth
my limbs, my body and feet,
beauty that men gasp
wondering that life
could rest in so burnt a face,
so scarred with her touch,
so fire-eaten, so intense.

Turn, for I love you yet,
though you are not worthy my love,
though you are not equal to it.

Turn back;
true I have glanced out
toward the purple ships
with seeming indifference.
I have fallen from the high grace
of the goddess,
for long days
I have been dulled with this grief,
but turn
before death strike,
for the goddess speaks:

She too is of the deathless,
she too will wander in my palaces
where all beauty is peace.

She too is of my host
that gather in groups or singly wait
by some altar apart;
she too is my poet.

Turn if you will
from her path,
turn if you must from her feet,
turn away, silent,
find rest if you wish:

find quiet
where the fir-trees
press, as you
swaying lightly above earth.

Turn if you will from her path
for one moment seek
a lesser beauty
and a lesser grace,
but you will find
no peace in the end
save in her presence.

Eros

I

Where is he taking us
now that he has turned back?

Where will this take us,
this fever,
spreading into light?

Nothing we have ever felt,
nothing we have dreamt,
or conjured in the night
or fashioned in loneliness,
can equal this.

Where is he taking us,
Eros,
now that he has turned back?

II

My mouth is wet with your life,
my eyes blinded with your face,
a heart itself which feels
the intimate music.

My mind is caught,
dimmed with it,
(where is love taking us?)
my lips are wet with your life.

In my body were pearls cast,
shot with Ionian tints, purple,
vivid through the white.

III

Keep love and he wings
with his bow,
up, mocking us,
keep love and he taunts us
and escapes.

Keep love and he sways apart

in another world,
outdistancing us.

Keep love and he mocks,
ah, bitter and sweet,
your sweetness is more cruel
than your hurt.

Honey and salt,
fire burst from the rocks
to meet fire
spilt from Hesperus.

Fire darted aloft and met fire,
and in that moment
love entered us.

IV

Could Eros be kept,
he was prisoned long since
and sick with imprisonment,
could Eros be kept,
others would have taken him
and crushed out his life.

Could Eros be kept,
we had sinned against the great god,
we too might have prisoned him outright.

Could Eros be kept,
nay, thank him and the bright goddess
that he left us.

V

Ah love is bitter and sweet,
but which is more sweet
the bitterness or the sweetness,
none has spoken it.

Love is bitter,
but can salt taint sea-flowers,
grief, happiness?

Is it bitter to give back
love to your lover if he crave it?

Is it bitter to give back
love to your lover if he wish it
for a new favourite,
who can say,
or is it sweet?

Is it sweet to possess utterly,
or is it bitter,
bitter as ash?

VI

I had thought myself frail,
a petal
with light equal
on leaf and under-leaf.

I had thought myself frail;
a lamp,
shell, ivory or crust of pearl,
about to fall shattered,
with flame spent.

I cried:

"I must perish,
I am deserted in this darkness,
an outcast, desperate,"
such fire rent me with Hesperus,

Then the day broke.

VII

What need of a lamp
when day lightens us,
what need to bind love
when love stands
with such radiant wings over us?

What need—
yet to sing love,
love must first shatter us.

Envy

I

I envy you your chance of death,
how I envy you this.
I am more covetous of him
even than of your glance,
I wish more from his presence
though he torture me in a grasp
terrible, intense.

Though he clasp me in an embrace
that is set against my will,
and rack me with his measure,
effortless yet full of strength,
and slay me
in that most horrible contest,
still, how I envy you your chance.

Though he pierce me with his lust,
iron, fever and dust,
though beauty is slain
when I perish,
I envy you death.

What is beauty to me?
has she not slain me enough,
have I not cried in agony of love,
birth, hate,
in pride crushed?

What is left after this?
what can death loose in me
after your embrace?
your touch,
your limbs are more terrible
to do me hurt.

What can death mar in me
that you have not?

II

What can death send me
that you have not?
You gathered violets,
you spoke:
"your hair is not less black
nor less fragrant,
nor in your eyes is less light,
your hair is not less sweet
with purple in the lift of locks;"
why were those slight words
and the violets you gathered
of such worth?

How I envy you death;
what could death bring,
more black, more set with sparks
to slay, to affright,
than the memory of those first violets,
the chance lift of your voice,
the chance blinding frenzy
as you bent?

III

Could I have known
you were more male than the sun-god,
more hot, more intense,
could I have known?
for your glance all-enfolding,
sympathetic, was selfless
as a girl's glance.

Could I have known?
I whose heart,
being rent, cared nothing,
was unspeakably indifferent.

IV

So the goddess has slain me
for your chance smile
and my scarf unfolding
as you stooped to it,
so she trapped me,
for the upward sweep of your arm,
as you lifted the veil,
was the gesture of a tall girl
and your smile was as selfless.

Could I have known?
nay, spare pity,
though I break,
crushed under the goddess' hate,
though I fall beaten at last,
so high have I thrust my glance
up into her presence.

Do not pity me, spare that,
but how I envy you
your chance of death.

Eurydice

I

So you have swept me back,
I who could have walked with the live souls
above the earth,
I who could have slept among the live flowers
at last;

so for your arrogance
and your ruthlessness
I am swept back
where dead lichens drip
dead cinders upon moss of ash;

so for your arrogance
I am broken at last,
I who had lived unconscious,
who was almost forgot;

if you had let me wait
I had grown from listlessness
into peace,
if you had let me rest with the dead,
I had forgot you
and the past.

II

Here only flame upon flame
and black among the red sparks,
streaks of black and light
grown colourless;

why did you turn back,
that hell should be reinhabited
of myself thus
swept into nothingness?

why did you turn?
why did you glance back?
why did you hesitate for that moment?
why did you bend your face
caught with the flame of the upper earth,
above my face?

what was it that crossed my face
with the light from yours
and your glance?
what was it you saw in my face?
the light of your own face,
the fire of your own presence?

What had my face to offer
but reflex of the earth,
hyacinth colour
caught from the raw fissure in the rock
where the light struck,
and the colour of azure crocuses
and the bright surface of gold crocuses
and of the wind-flower,
swift in its veins as lightning
and as white.

III

Saffron from the fringe of the earth,
wild saffron that has bent
over the sharp edge of earth,
all the flowers that cut through the earth,
all, all the flowers are lost;

everything is lost,
everything is crossed with black,
black upon black
and worse than black,
this colourless light.

IV

Fringe upon fringe
of blue crocuses,
crocuses, walled against blue of themselves,
blue of that upper earth,
blue of the depth upon depth of flowers,
lost;

flowers,
if I could have taken once my breath of them,
enough of them,
more than earth,
even than of the upper earth,
had passed with me
beneath the earth;

if I could have caught up from the earth,
the whole of the flowers of the earth,
if once I could have breathed into myself
the very golden crocuses
and the red,
and the very golden hearts of the first saffron,
the whole of the golden mass,
the whole of the great fragrance,
I could have dared the loss.

V

So for your arrogance
and your ruthlessness
I have lost the earth
and the flowers of the earth,
and the live souls above the earth,
and you who passed across the light
and reached
ruthless;

you who have your own light,

who are to yourself a presence,
who need no presence;

yet for all your arrogance
and your glance,
I tell you this:

such loss is no loss,
such terror, such coils and strands and pitfalls
of blackness,
such terror
is no loss;

hell is no worse than your earth
above the earth,
hell is no worse,
no, nor your flowers
nor your veins of light
nor your presence,
a loss;

my hell is no worse than yours
though you pass among the flowers and speak
with the spirits above earth.

VI

Against the black
I have more fervour
than you in all the splendour of that place,
against the blackness
and the stark grey
I have more light;

and the flowers,
if I should tell you,
you would turn from your own fit paths
toward hell,
turn again and glance back

and I would sink into a place
even more terrible than this.

VII

At least I have the flowers of myself,
and my thoughts, no god
can take that;
I have the fervour of myself for a presence
and my own spirit for light;

and my spirit with its loss
knows this;
though small against the black,
small against the formless rocks,
hell must break before I am lost;

before I am lost,
hell must open like a red rose
for the dead to pass.

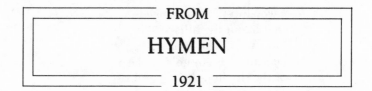

Hippolytus Temporizes

I worship the greatest first—
(it were sweet, the couch,
the brighter ripple of cloth
over the dipped fleece;
the thought: her bones
under the flesh are white
as sand which along a beach
covers but keeps the print
of the crescent shapes beneath:
I thought:
between cloth and fleece,
so her body lies.)

I worship first, the great—
(ah, sweet, your eyes—
what God, invoked in Crete,
gave them the gift to part
as the Sidonian myrtle-flower
suddenly, wide and swart,
then swiftly,
the eye-lids having provoked our hearts—
as suddenly beat and close.)

I worship the feet, flawless,
that haunt the hills—
(ah, sweet, dare I think,
beneath fetter of golden clasp,
of the rhythm, the fall and rise
of yours, carven, slight
beneath straps of gold that keep
their slender beauty caught,
like wings and bodies
of trapped birds.)

I worship the greatest first—
(suddenly into my brain—
the flash of sun on the snow,
the fringe of light and the drift,
the crest and the hill-shadow—
ah, surely now I forget,
ah splendour, my goddess turns:
or was it the sudden heat,
beneath quivering of molten flesh,
of veins, purple as violets?)

The Islands

I

What are the islands to me,
what is Greece,
what is Rhodes, Samos, Chios,
what is Paros facing west,
what is Crete?

What is Samothrace,
rising like a ship,
what is Imbros rending the storm-waves
with its breast?

What is Naxos, Paros, Milos,
what the circle about Lycia,
what, the Cyclades'
white necklace?

What is Greece—
Sparta, rising like a rock,
Thebes, Athens,
what is Corinth?

What is Euboia
with its island violets,
what is Euboia, spread with grass,
set with swift shoals,
what is Crete?

What are the islands to me,
what is Greece?

II

What can love of land give to me
that you have not—
what do the tall Spartans know,
and gentler Attic folk?

What has Sparta and her women
more than this?

What are the islands to me
if you are lost—
what is Naxos, Tinos, Andros,
and Delos, the clasp
of the white necklace?

III

What can love of land give to me
that you have not,

what can love of strife break in me
that you have not?

Though Sparta enter Athens,
Thebes wrack Sparta,
each changes as water,
salt, rising to wreak terror
and fall back.

IV

"What has love of land given to you
that I have not?"

I have questioned Tyrians
where they sat
on the black ships,
weighted with rich stuffs,
I have asked the Greeks
from the white ships,
and Greeks from ships whose hulks
lay on the wet sand, scarlet
with great beaks.
I have asked bright Tyrians
and tall Greeks—
"what has love of land given you?"
And they answered—"peace."

V

But beauty is set apart,
beauty is cast by the sea,
a barren rock,
beauty is set about
with wrecks of ships,
upon our coast, death keeps
the shallows—death waits
clutching toward us
from the deeps.

Beauty is set apart;
the winds that slash its beach,
swirl the coarse sand
upward toward the rocks.

Beauty is set apart
from the islands
and from Greece.

VI

In my garden
the winds have beaten
the ripe lilies;
in my garden, the salt
has wilted the first flakes
of young narcissus,
and the lesser hyacinth,
and the salt has crept
under the leaves of the white hyacinth.

In my garden
even the wind-flowers lie flat,
broken by the wind at last.

VII

What are the islands to me
if you are lost,
what is Paros to me
if your eyes draw back,
what is Milos
if you take fright of beauty,
terrible, torturous, isolated,
a barren rock?

What is Rhodes, Crete,
what is Paros facing west,
what, white Imbros?

What are the islands to me
if you hesitate,
what is Greece if you draw back
from the terror
and cold splendour of song
and its bleak sacrifice?

Fragment 113

"Neither honey nor bee for me."—Sappho.

Not honey,
not the plunder of the bee
from meadow or sand-flower
or mountain bush;
from winter-flower or shoot
born of the later heat:
not honey, not the sweet
stain on the lips and teeth:
not honey, not the deep
plunge of soft belly
and the clinging of the gold-edged
pollen-dusted feet;

not so—
though rapture blind my eyes,
and hunger crisp
dark and inert my mouth,
not honey, not the south,
not the tall stalk
of red twin-lilies,
nor light branch of fruit tree
caught in flexible light branch;

not honey, not the south;
ah flower of purple iris,

flower of white,
or of the iris, withering the grass—
for fleck of the sun's fire,
gathers such heat and power,
that shadow-print is light,
cast through the petals
of the yellow iris flower;

not iris—old desire—old passion—
old forgetfulness—old pain—
not this, nor any flower,
but if you turn again,
seek strength of arm and throat,
touch as the god;
neglect the lyre-note;
knowing that you shall feel,
about the frame,
no trembling of the string
but heat, more passionate
of bone and the white shell
and fiery tempered steel.

Helen

All Greece hates
the still eyes in the white face,
the lustre as of olives
where she stands,
and the white hands.

All Greece reviles
the wan face when she smiles,
hating it deeper still
when it grows wan and white,
remembering past enchantments
and past ills.

Greece sees unmoved,
God's daughter, born of love,
the beauty of cool feet
and slenderest knees,
could love indeed the maid,
only if she were laid,
white ash amid funereal cypresses.

Fragment Thirty-six

I know not what to do:
my mind is divided.—Sappho.

I know not what to do,
my mind is reft:
is song's gift best?
is love's gift loveliest?
I know not what to do,
now sleep has pressed
weight on your eyelids.

Shall I break your rest,
devouring, eager?
is love's gift best?
nay, song's the loveliest:
yet were you lost,
what rapture
could I take from song?
what song were left?

I know not what to do:
to turn and slake
the rage that burns,
with my breath burn
and trouble your cool breath?
so shall I turn and take
snow in my arms?
(is love's gift best?)
yet flake on flake
of snow were comfortless,
did you lie wondering,
wakened yet unawake.

Shall I turn and take
comfortless snow within my arms?
press lips to lips
that answer not,

press lips to flesh
that shudders not nor breaks?

Is love's gift best?
shall I turn and slake
all the wild longing?
O I am eager for you!
as the Pleiads shake
white light in whiter water
so shall I take you?

My mind is quite divided,
my minds hesitate,
so perfect matched,
I know not what to do:
each strives with each
as two white wrestlers
standing for a match,
ready to turn and clutch
yet never shake muscle nor nerve nor tendon;
so my mind waits
to grapple with my mind,
yet I lie quiet,
I would seem at rest.

I know not what to do:
strain upon strain,
sound surging upon sound
makes my brain blind;
as a wave-line may wait to fall
yet (waiting for its falling)
still the wind may take
from off its crest,
white flake on flake of foam,
that rises,
seeming to dart and pulse
and rend the light,
so my mind hesitates
above the passion

quivering yet to break,
so my mind hesitates
above my mind,
listening to song's delight.

I know not what to do:
will the sound break,
rending the night
with rift on rift of rose
and scattered light?
will the sound break at last
as the wave hesitant,
or will the whole night pass
and I lie listening awake?

Cassandra

O Hymen king.

Hymen, O Hymen king,
what bitter thing is this?
what shaft, tearing my heart?
what scar, what light, what fire
searing my eye-balls and my eyes with flame?
nameless, O spoken name,
king, lord, speak blameless Hymen.

Why do you blind my eyes?
why do you dart and pulse
till all the dark is home,
then find my soul
and ruthless draw it back?
scaling the scaleless,
opening the dark?
speak, nameless, power and might;
when will you leave me quite?

when will you break my wings
or leave them utterly free
to scale heaven endlessly?

A bitter, broken thing,
my heart, O Hymen lord,
yet neither drought nor sword
baffles men quite,
why must they feign to fear
my virgin glance?
feigned utterly or real
why do they shrink?
my trance frightens them,
breaks the dance,
empties the market-place;
if I but pass they fall
back, frantically;
must always people mock?
unless they shrink and reel
as in the temple
at your uttered will.

O Hymen king,
lord, greatest, power, might,
look for my face is dark,
burnt with your light,
your fire, O Hymen lord;
is there none left
can equal me
in ecstasy, desire?
is there none left
can bear with me
the kiss of your white fire?
is there not one,
Phrygian or frenzied Greek,
poet, song-swept, or bard,
one meet to take from me

this bitter power of song,
one fit to speak, Hymen,
your praises, lord?

May I not wed
as you have wed?
may it not break, beauty,
from out my hands, my head, my feet?
may Love not lie beside me
till his heat
burn me to ash?
may he not comfort me, then,
spent of all that fire and heat,
still, ashen-white and cool
as the wet laurels,
white, before your feet
step on the mountain-slope,
before your fiery hand
lift up the mantle
covering flower and land,
as a man lifts,
O Hymen, from his bride,
(cowering with woman eyes,) the veil?
O Hymen lord, be kind.

Toward the Piraeus

Slay with your eyes, Greek,
men over the face of the earth,
slay with your eyes, the host,
puny, passionless, weak.

Break as the ranks of steel
broke when the Persian lost:

craven, we hated them then:
now we would count them Gods
beside these, spawn of the earth.

Grant us your mantle, Greek!
grant us but one
to fright (as your eyes) with a sword,
men, craven and weak,
grant us but one to strike
one blow for you, passionate Greek.

1

You would have broken my wings,
but the very fact that you knew
I had wings, set some seal
on my bitter heart, my heart
broke and fluttered and sang.

You would have snared me,
and scattered the strands of my nest;
but the very fact that you saw,
sheltered me, claimed me,
set me apart from the rest

Of men—of *men*, made you a god,
and me, claimed me, set me apart
and the song in my breast,
yours, yours forever—
if I escape your evil heart.

2

I loved you:
men have writ and women have said
they loved,
but as the Pythoness stands by the altar,
intense and may not move,

till the fumes pass over;
and may not falter or break,
till the priest has caught the words
that mar or make
a deme or a ravaged town;

so I, though my knees tremble,
my heart break,
must note the rumbling,
heed only the shuddering
down in the fissure beneath the rock
of the temple floor;

must wait and watch
and may not turn nor move,
nor break from my trance to speak
so slight, so sweet,
so simple a word as love.

3

What had you done
had you been true,
I can not think,
I may not know.

What could we do
were I not wise,
what play invent,
what joy devise?

What could we do
if you were great?

(Yet were you lost,
who were there then,
to circumvent
the tricks of men?)

What can we do,
for curious lies
have filled your heart,
and in my eyes
sorrow has writ
that I am wise.

4

If I had been a boy,
I would have worshipped your grace,
I would have flung my worship
before your feet,
I would have followed apart,
glad, rent with an ecstasy
to watch you turn
your great head, set on the throat,
thick, dark with its sinews,
burned and wrought
like the olive stalk,
and the noble chin
and the throat.

I would have stood,
and watched and watched
and burned,
and when in the night,
from the many hosts, your slaves,
and warriors and serving men
you had turned
to the purple couch and the flame
of the woman, tall like the cypress tree
that flames sudden and swift and free
as with crackle of golden resin
and cones and the locks flung free
like the cypress limbs,
bound, caught and shaken and loosed,
bound, caught and riven and bound

and loosened again,
as in rain of a kingly storm
or wind full from a desert plain.

So, when you had risen
from all the lethargy of love and its heat,
you would have summoned me,
me alone,
and found my hands,
beyond all the hands in the world,
cold, cold, cold,
intolerably cold and sweet.

5

It was not chastity that made me cold nor fear,
only I knew that you, like myself, were sick
of the puny race that crawls and quibbles and lisps
of love and love and lovers and love's deceit.

It was not chastity that made me wild, but fear
that my weapon, tempered in different heat,
was over-matched by yours, and your hand
skilled to yield death-blows, might break

With the slightest turn—no ill will meant—
my own lesser, yet still somewhat fine-wrought,
fiery-tempered, delicate, over-passionate steel.

Let Zeus Record

I

I say, I am quite done,
quite done with this;
you smile your calm
inveterate chill smile

and light steps back;
intolerate loveliness
smiles at the ranks
of obdurate bitterness;

you smile with keen
chiselled and frigid lips;
it seems no evil
ever could have been;

so, on the Parthenon,
like splendour keeps
peril at bay,
facing inviolate dawn.

II

Men cannot mar you,
women cannot break
your innate strength,
your stark autocracy;

still I will make no plea
for this slight verse;
it outlines simply
Love's authority:

but pardon this,
that in these luminous days,
I re-invoke the dark
to frame your praise;

as one to make a bright room
seem more bright,
stares out deliberate
into Cerberus-night.

III

Sometimes I chide the manner of your dress;
I want all men to see the grace of you;
I mock your pace, your body's insolence,
thinking that all should praise, while obstinate
you still insist your beauty's gold is clay:

I chide you that you stand not forth entire,
set on bright plinth, intolerably desired;
yet I in turn will cheat, will thwart your whim,
I'll break my thought, weld it to fit your measure
as one who sets a statue on a height
to show where Hyacinth or Pan have been.

IV

When blight lay and the Persian like a scar,
and death was heavy on Athens, plague and war,
you gave me this bright garment and this ring;

I who still kept of wisdom's meagre store
a few rare songs and some philosophising,
offered you these for I had nothing more;

that which both Athens and the Persian mocked
you took, as a cold famished bird takes grain,
blown inland through darkness and withering rain.

V

Would you prefer myrrh-flower or cyclamen?
I have them, I could spread them out again;
but now for this stark moment while Love breathes
his tentative breath, as dying, yet still lives,
wait as that time you waited tense with me:

others shall love when Athens lives again,
you waited in the agonies of war;
others will praise when all the host proclaims
Athens the perfect; you, when Athens lost,
stood by her; when the dark perfidious host
turned, it was you who pled for her with death.

VI

Stars wheel in purple, yours is not so rare
as Hesperus, nor yet so great a star
as bright Aldebaran or Sirius,
nor yet the stained and brilliant one of War;

stars turn in purple, glorious to the sight;
yours is not gracious as the Pleiads' are
nor as Orion's sapphires, luminous;

yet disenchanted, cold, imperious face,
when all the others, blighted, reel and fall,
your star, steel-set, keeps lone and frigid tryst
to freighted ships, baffled in wind and blast.

VII

None watched with me
who watched his fluttering breath,
none brought white roses,
none the roses red;

many had loved,
had sought him luminous,
when he was blithe
and purple draped his bed;

yet when Love fell
struck down with plague and war,
you lay white myrrh-buds
on the darkened lintel;

you fastened blossom
to the smitten sill;
let Zeus record this,
daring Death to mar.

Epitaph

So I may say,
"I died of living,
having lived one hour";

so they may say,
"she died soliciting
illicit fervour";

so you may say,
"Greek flower; Greek ecstasy
reclaims for ever

one who died
following
intricate songs' lost measure."

The Mysteries

Renaissance Choros

Dark
days are past
and darker days draw near;
darkness on this side,
darkness over there
threatens the spirit
like massed hosts
a sheer
handful
of thrice-doomed spearsmen;
enemy this side,
enemy a part
of hill
and mountain-crest
and under-hill;
nothing before of mystery,
nothing past,
only the emptiness,
pitfall of death,
terror,
the flood,
the earthquake,
stormy ill;
then voice within the turmoil,

that slight breath
that tells as one flower may
of winter past
(that kills
with Pythian bow,
the Delphic pest;)
one flower,
slight voice,
reveals
all holiness
with
"peace
be still."

II

A sceptre
and a flower-shaft
and a spear,
one flower may kill the winter,
so this rare
enchanter
and magician
and arch-mage;
one flower may slay the winter
and meet death,
so this
goes and returns
and dies
and comes to bless
again,
again;
a sceptre and a flower
and a near
protector
to the lost and impotent;
yea,
I am lost,
behold what star is near;

yea,
I am weak,
see
what enchanted armour
clothes the intrepid mind
that sheds the gear
of blighting thought;
behold what wit is here
what subtlety,
what humour
and what light;
see,
I am done,
no lover and none dear,
a voice within the fever,
that slight breath
belies our terror
and our hopelessness,
"lo,
I am here."

III

"Not to destroy,
nay, but to sanctify
the flower
that springs
Adonis
from the dead;
behold,
behold
the lilies
how they grow,
behold how fair,
behold how pure a red,
(so love has died)
behold the lilies
bled
for love;

not emperor nor ruler,
none may claim
such splendour;
king may never boast
so beautiful a garment
as the host
of field
and mountain lilies."

IV

"Not to destroy,
nay, but to sanctify
each flame
that springs
upon the brow of Love;
not to destroy
but to re-invoke
and name
afresh each flower,
serpent
and bee
and bird;
behold,
behold
the spotted snake
how wise;
behold the dove,
the sparrow,
not one dies
without your father;
man sets the trap
and bids the arrow fly,
man snares the mother-bird
while passing by
the shivering fledglings,
leaving them to lie
starving;
no man,

no man,
no man
may ever fear
that this one,
winnowing the lovely air,
is overtaken by a bird of prey,
that this is stricken
in its wild-wood plight,
that this dies broken
in the wild-wood snare,
I
and my father
care."

V

"Not to destroy,
nay, but to sanctify
the fervour
of all ancient mysteries;
behold the dead are lost,
the grass has lain
trampled
and stained
and sodden;
behold,
behold,
behold
the grass disdains
the rivulet
of snow and mud and rain;
the grass,
the grass
rises
with flower-bud;
the grain
lifts its bright spear-head
to the sun again;
behold,

behold
the dead
are no more dead,
the grain is gold,
blade,
stalk
and seed within;
the mysteries
are in the grass
and rain."

VI

"The mysteries remain,
I keep the same
cycle of seed-time
and of sun and rain;
Demeter in the grass
I multiply,
renew and bless
Iacchus in the vine;
I hold the law,
I keep the mysteries true,
the first of these
to name the living, dead;
I am red wine and bread.

I keep the law,
I hold the mysteries true,
I am the vine,
the branches, you
and you."

Magician

1

There is no man can take,
there is no pool can slake,
ultimately I am alone;
ultimately I am done;

I say,
take colour;
break white into red,
into blue
into violet
into green;
I say,
take each separately,
the white will slay;

pray constantly,
give me green, Artemis,
red, Ares,
blue, Aphrodite, true lover,
or rose;
I say, look at the lawns,
how the spray
of clematis makes gold or the ray
of the delphinium

violet;
I say,
worship each separate;
no man can endure
your intolerable radium;

white,
radiant,
pure;
who are you?
we are unsure;
give us back the old gods,
to make your plight
tolerable;

pull out the nails,
fling them aside,
any old boat,
left at high-tide,
(you yourself would admit)
has iron as pliable;

burn the thorn;
thorn burns;
how it crackles;
you yourself would be the first to seek
dried weed by some high-sand
to make the land
liveable;

you yourself;
would be the first to scrap
the old trophies
for new.

2

We have crawled back into the womb;
you command?
be born again,

be born,
be born;
the sand
turns gold ripple and the blue
under-side of the wrasse
glints radium-violet as it leaps;
the dolphin leaves a new track,
the bird cuts new wing-beat,
the fox burrows,
begets;
the rabbit,
the ferret,
the weasel,
the stoat and the newt
have nests;
you said,
the foxes have holes,
you yourself none,
do you ask us
to creep in the earth?

too long, too long,
O my Lord,
have we crept,
too long, too long, O my King
have we slept,
too long have we slain,
too long have we wept.

3

What is fire upon rain?
colour;
what is dew upon grass?
odour;
what are you upon us?
fragrance of honey-locust.

What man is cursed?
he without lover;

what woman is blasphemous?
she who, under cover of your cloak,
casts love out.

Your cloak hides the sinner,
your cloak shields the lover,
colour of wine,
cyclamen,
red rhododendron.

4

Salt, salt the kiss
of beauty where Love is,
salt, salt the refrain,
beat, beat again,
say again,
again,
Beauty,
our King
is slain;

beautiful the hands,
beautiful the feet,
the thighs beautiful;

O is it right,
is it meet?
we have dared too long to worship
an idol,
to worship drab sack-cloth,
to worship dead candles;
light the candles, sing;
tear down every effigy, for none has granted
him beauty;

too long,
too long in the dark,
the sea howls,
and the wind,

a shark rises
to tear
teeth, jaws; revels in horrors;
too long, too long,
have we propitiated the terror in the sea,
forgotten its beauty.

5

I instil rest;
there is no faith and no hope
without sleep;
the poppy-seed is alive to wake
you to another world,
take:
take the poppy-seed,
one grain has more worth than fields of ripe grain or
    barley,

no yield of a thousand and thousand measure,
baskets piled up and pressed down,
no measure running over, can yield
such treasure;

He said,
consider the flower of the field;

did he specify
blue or red?

6

Too long we prayed
God in the thunder,
wonderful though he be
and our father;

too long, too long in the rain,
cowering lest he strike again;

showering peril,
disclosing our evil;

He was right, we knew;
so we fled
him in rocks,
cowered from the Power overhead,
ate grass like the ox;

we will submit;
yes, we bled,
cut ourselves to propitiate
his wrath;

for we asked,
what, what awaits us,
once dead?

we never heard the Magician
we never, never heard what he said.

7

We expected some gesture,
some actor-logic,
some turn of the head,
he spoke simply;
we had followed the priest and the answering word
of the people;

to this,
was no answer;

we expected some threat or some promise,
some disclosure,
we were not as these others;

but he spoke to the rabble;
dead,

dead,
dead were our ears
that heard not, yet heard.

8

A basket,
a fish
or fish net,
the knot of the cord
that fastens the boat,
the oar
or the rudder,
the board or the sail-cloth,
the wind as it lifts sand and grass,
the grass
and the flower in the grass;

the grape,
the grape-leaf,
the half-opened tendril,
the red grape, the white grape, the blue grape,
the size of the wood-vine stock,
its roots in the earth,
its bark and its contour,
the shape of the olive,
the goat,
the kid and the lamb,
the sheep,
the shepherd,
his wood-pipe,
his hound,
the wild-bird,
the bird untrapped,
the bird sold in the market;

the laying of fish on the embers,
the taste of the fish,
the feel of the texture of bread,
the round and the half-loaf,

the grain of a petal,
the rain-bow and the rain;

he named these things simply;
sat down at our table,
stood,
named salt,
called to a friend;

he named herbs and simples,
what garnish?
a fine taste,
he called for some ripe wine;

peeled a plum,
remembered the brass bowl
lest he stain
our host's towel;

was courteous,
not over-righteous;
why—
a girl came where he sat,
flung a rose from a basket,
and one broke
a fine box
of Cyprian ivory,
(or alabaster)
a rare scent.

9

He liked jewels,
the fine feel of white pearls;
he would lift a pearl from a tray,
flatter an Ethiopian merchant
on his taste;
lift crystal from Syria,
to the light;

he would see worlds in a crystal
and while we waited for a camel
or a fine Roman's litter
to crowd past,
he would tell of the whorl of whorl of light
that was infinity to be seen in glass,

or a shell
or a bead
or a pearl.

From Sigil

XI

If you take the moon in your hands
and turn it round
(heavy, slightly tarnished platter)
you're there;

if you pull dry sea-weed from the sand
and turn it round
and wonder at the underside's bright amber,
your eyes

look out as they did here,
(you don't remember)
when my soul turned round,

perceiving the other-side of everything,
mullein-leaf, dog-wood leaf, moth-wing
and dandelion-seed under the ground.

XII

Are these ashes in my hand
or a wand
to conjure a butterfly

out of a nest,
a dragon-fly
out of a leaf,

a moon-flower
from a flower husk,

or fire-flies
from a thicket?

XIV

Now let the cycle sweep us here and there,
we will not struggle,
somewhere,
under a forest-ledge,
a wild white-pear
will blossom;

somewhere,
under an edge of rock,
a sea will open;
slice of the tide-shelf
will show in coral, yourself,
in conch-shell,
myself;

somewhere,
over a field-hedge,
a wild bird
will lift up wild, wild throat,
and that song heard,
will stifle out this note
and this song note.

XV

So if you love me,
love me everywhere,
blind to all argument

or phantasy,
claim the one signet;

truly in the sky,
God marked me to be his,
scrawled, "I, I, I
alone can comprehend

this subtlety":
a song is very simple
or is bound
with inter-woven complicated sound;

one undertakes
the song's integrity,
another all the filament
wound round

chord and discord,
the quarter-note and whole
run of iambic
or of coryamb:

"no one can grasp,"
(God wrote)
"nor understand
the two, insolvent,
only he and you";

shall we two witness
that his writ is wise
or shall we rise,

wing-tip to purple wing,
create new earth,
new skies?

XVI

But it won't be that way,

I'm sane,
normal again;

I'm sane,
normal as when
we last sat in this room
with other people who spoke
pleasant speakable things;

though
you lifted your brow
as a sun-parched branch to the rain,
and I lifted my soul
as from the northern gloom,
an ice-flower to the sun,
they didn't know

how
my heart woke
to a range and measure
of song
I hadn't known;

as yours spoke through your eyes,
I recalled
a trivial little joke we had,
lest the others see
how the walls stretched out
to desert and sand,
the Symplegedes
and the sea.

XVII

Time breaks the barrier,
we are on a reef,
wave lengthens on to sand,
sand keeps wave-beat

furrowed in its heart,

so keep print of my hand;
you are the sea-surge,
lift me from the land,

let me be swept out in you,
let me slake the last,
last ultimate thirst;
I am you;

you are cursed;
men have cursed God,
let me be no more man,
God has cursed man,

let me go out and sink
into the ultimate sleep;
take me,
let your hand

gather my throat,
flower from that land
we both have loved,
have lost;

O wand of ebony, keep away the night,
O ivory wand,
bring back the ultimate light
on Delphic headland;

take me,
O ultimate breath,
O master-lyrist,
beat my wild heart to death.

XVIII

Are we unfathomable night
with the new moon
to give it depth

and carry vision further,
or are we rather stupid,
marred with feeling?

will we gain all things,
being over-fearful,
or will we lose the clue,
miss out the sense
of all the scrawled script,
being over-careful?

is each one's reticence
the other's food,
or is this mood
sheer poison to the other?

how do I know
what pledge you gave your God,
how do you know
who is my Lord
and Lover?

XIX

"I love you,"
spoken in rhapsodic metre,
leaves me cold:

I have a horror
of finality,
I would rather
hazard a guess,
wonder whether
either of us
could for a moment
endure the other,
after the first fine flavour
of irony
had worn off.

Calypso

I

CALYPSO
(*perceiving
the long-wandering
Odysseus, clamber-
ing ashore*)

Clumsy futility, drown yourself—
did I ask you to this rock-shelf,
did I lure you here?
did I call, far and near,
*come, come Odysseus,
you, you, you alone
are the unmatchable mate,
my own?*
sea-nymph may sing;
I didn't say anything
even to the air;
I was alone,
bound hair,
unbound
and let it fall,
wound in no fillet nor any pearl
nor coral,
only nodded
peaceful things;
I asked no wings
to lift me to mid-heaven,
to drop me to earth;
I was alone
now
my beautiful peace has gone;

did I ask you here?
O laugh, most intimate waters,
little cove
and the answering ripples
of the spring
that sends clear water to the salt,
tell me,
did I whisper to you ought

that would work a charm?
did I, unwittingly,
invoke some swallow
to fly low,
to beat into the hollow
of those great eyes,
stupid as an ox,
wide with surprise?
did I? did I?
I am priestess, occult, nymph
        and goddess,
then what was my fault?
there must have been fault
        somewhere,
in the wind,
in the air,
some counter-trick
to mock magic,
some counter-smile
some malign goddess
to smile awry,

O see, Calypso, poor girl,
is caught at last;

O oaf, O ass,
O any slow, plodding and silly
        animal,
O man,
I am amused to think you may
        fall;
here where I feel
maiden-hair,
where I clutch the root of the
        sea-bay,
where I slide a thin foot along
a crack,
you will slip;

you are heavy,
great oaf,
walrus,
whale, clumsy on land,
clumsy with your great arms
        with an oar
at sea;
you have no wit in the air,
you are fit only to clamber
to climb, then to fall;
then to fall;
you will slide clumsy
unto the sand.

ODYSSEUS

On land, I know my way
as well as by sea,
she who is light as a bird,
who shouts wilful words
back to me,
shall know,
Odysseus is at home;
witness O land,
O rock,
O little fern that is torn here,
where my hand
fondles the rock,
to set back the torn root,
O shoot of bay-tree, here
a hand tore
a leaf,
leaf is scattered,
a shredded branch
lies below on the shore
making a letter;
I lean forward to read—alpha? it
        must be—
well begin then—
climb higher—

what letter did the branch make?
omega—the end?
a snake, wound to a cypher,
nothing, nothing for you
O land-lover,
but to follow;
Odysseus,
climb higher!

CALYPSO

Idiot;
did he think he could reach the
    ledge?
why, already he leans over the
    edge;
he is dizzy,
he will fall—
shout, shout O sea-gulls,
large pickings for the wrasse,
    the eel;
we eat Odysseus, the land-walrus
to-morrow with parsley
and bean-sauce—
eat,
that's what I could do;
eat fruit—
drink deep from crystal bowl—

ODYSSEUS

Where has she flown?
ah, a wild-plum branch has
    caught—
what?
the gilt clasp of a sandal?
vanity for a nymph—
a nymph is a woman—

CALYPSO
(*below in
the cave*)

What is that?

ODYSSEUS	Ah, I see, a narrow track concealed, and not too carefully.
CALYPSO	Isn't he drowned yet?
ODYSSEUS (*peers down*)	There she is under the ground.
CALYPSO (*in the* *cave*)	Now I am free; no one can find, no one can follow—
ODYSSEUS	—but me.

CALYPSO	Vision of obscene force
	what brought you here?
	away—
	evil goddesses of the west,
	I will counter-provoke the
	    elements—
	will flood your shallow sands
	    with sea-water—
	my father—

ODYSSEUS	Your father?
CALYPSO	A king, a god— owner of ocean—
ODYSSEUS (*clasps her*)	All men are fathers, kings and gods—
CALYPSO	Too soon—O hound— beast of an insensitive pack— you can not take me that way—
ODYSSEUS	A nymph is a woman.

CALYPSO	No human to weep like your Greek—
ODYSSEUS	Laugh then.
CALYPSO	Not at the command of men.
ODYSSEUS	You will do as I say— why did you wear sandals like a woman, if you are not human?
CALYPSO	I am half of the air— the rocks hurt my feet—
ODYSSEUS (*drops her*)	Beware— you will moan soon that you are not all woman.
CALYPSO (*her hair spread on his chest. He sleeps*)	What did he say? O you gods— O you gods— he shall never get away.

II

CALYPSO (*on land*)	O you clouds, here is my song; man is clumsy and evil, a devil. O you sand, this is my command, drown all men in slow breathless suffocation— then they may understand.

O you winds,
beat his sails flat,
shift a wave sideways
that he suffocate.

O you waves,
run counter to his oars,
waft him to blistering shores,
where he may die of thirst.

O you skies,
send rain
to wash salt from my eyes,

and witness all earth and heaven,
it was of my heart-blood
his sails were woven;
witness, river and sea and land;
you, you must hear me—
man is a devil,
man will not understand.

ODYSSEUS
(*on the sea*)

She gave me fresh water in an
      earth-jar,
strange fruits
to quench thirst,
a golden zither
to work magic on the water;

she gave me wine in a cup
and white wine in a crystal shell;
she gave me water and salt,
wrapped in a palm leaf
and palm-dates:

she gave me wool and a pelt of
      fur,

she gave me a pelt of silver-fox,
and a brown soft skin of a bear,

she gave me an ivory comb for
        my hair,
she washed brine and mud from
        my body,
and cool hands
held balm
for a rust-wound;

she gave me water
and fruit in a basket,
and shallow
baskets of pulse and grain, and
        a ball
of hemp
for mending the sail;

she gave me a willow basket
for letting into the shallows
for eels;

she gave me peace in her cave.

CALYPSO
(*from land*)
He has gone,
he has forgotten;
he took my lute and my shell of
        crystal—
he never looked back—

ODYSSEUS
(*on the sea*)
She gave me a wooden flute,
and a mantle,
she wove of this wool—

CALYPSO
(*from land*)
—for man is a brute and a fool.

The Dancer

I

I came far,
you came far,
both from strange cities,
I from the west,
you from the east;

but distance can not mar
nor deter
meeting, when fire meets
ice or ice
fire;

which is which?
either is either;
you are a witch,
you rise out of nowhere,
the boards you tread on,
are transferred
to Asia Minor;

you come from some walled town,
you bring its sorcery with you;
I am a priestess,
I am a priest;
you are a priest,
you are a priestess;
I am a devote of Hecate,
crouched by a deep jar
that contains herb,
pulse and white-bean,
red-bean and unknown small leek-stalk and grass blade;

I worship nature,
you are nature.

I worship art;
I am now from the city
of thinkers, of wisdom-makers,
and I watch as one come from afar
in a silver robe;

I carry no wine-jar;

I watch intent,
as one outside with whom is the answer;
intelligence alert,
I am here to report,
to say this is
or is not
God;

I am perfectly aware,
perfectly cold;

a girl clutches her lover's wrist,
I do not care,
(I am perfectly aware of what you are doing,
of what seeds you are sowing)
I know what this youth thinks,
what nerve throbs in that old man,
how that wan soldier
back from the last war,
feels healing, electric, in a clear bar,
where an arm should be;

nothing is hidden
from me;

if you make one false move,
I will slay you;
I hate and have no fear,
you can not betray me,

you can not betray us,
not the Sun,
who is your Lord;

for you are abstract,
making no mistake,
slurring no word
in the rhythm you make,
the poem,
writ in the air.

III

Fair,
fair,
fair,
do we deserve beauty?
pure,
pure,
fire,
do we dare
follow desire
where you show
perfection?

loveliest,
O strong,
ember
burns in ice,
snow folds over ember;
fire flashes through clear ice,
pattern frozen is red-rose,
rhododendrons bend under full snow,
yet each flower retains colour;

the rhododendrons are in flower
and snow covers
the flame heat
of purple,
of crimson,

of dark-blue,
of pale-blue,
of white
crystal
calyx;

miracle,
miracle of beauty returned to us,
the sun
born in a woman.

IV

We are more than human,
following your flame,
O woman;

we are more than fire,
following your controlled
vibrance;

we are more than ice,
listening to the slow
beat of our hearts,
like under-current of sap in a flowering tree,
covered with late snow;

we are more than we know.

V

Give us the strength to follow,
the power to hallow
beauty;

you are wind in a stark tree,
you are the stark tree unbent,
you are a strung bow,
you are an arrow,
another arrow;

your feet fling their arrows,
your twin arrows,
you then pulse into one flame;
O luminous,
your feet melt into folded wing,
to mer-maid's tail;

O love in the circle
of opening,
of closing,
of opening;

you are every colour of butterfly,
now in a frail robe, you are a white butterfly;
burning with white fervour,
you are moon-flower,
seen in water.

VI

You are every flower,
I can not stop to name;
nor do I claim
precedence among the harp-players;
my song-note falters;

I claim no precedence among the flute-players,
for I could not maintain
presence enough to stand,
there at your feet
with the rest,
making that music;

I can not name
the Doric nor the Ionic
measure,
nor claim greatness;
I have gained
no laurel
at Delphi;

but he,
your Father,
burning sun-lover
has yet had his jest,
has said, among all these
there is one voice,
one councillor;

listen,
Rhodocleia,

he says;

"dance for the world is dead,
dance for you are my mistress,
you are my stylus,
you write in the air with this foot,
with that foot,
with this arrow;
your flung hand
is that pointed arrow,
your taut frame
is one arrow,
my message;

you are my arrow,
my flame;
I have sent you into the world;
beside you,
men may name
no other;
you will never die;

nor this one,
whom you see not,
sitting, sullen and silent,
this poet."

O let us never meet, my love,
let us never clasp hands
as man and woman,
as woman and man,
as woman and woman,
as man and man;

O let us never speak, my love,
let us never utter
words less than my heart-beat,
words less than your throbbing feet;

white cygnet,
black missel-thrush,

let us never crush
breast to breast,
let us never rush
purple to purple fire,
wide flowers,
crushed under the glory
of god in the whirl-wind,
of god in the torrent;

O chaste Aphrodite,

let us be wild and free,
let us retain integrity,
intensity,
taut as the bow,
the Pythian strings
to slay sorrow.

VIII

There is much to know
and little time,
O bright arrow;

there are many to heal
and few to feel
the majesty
of our King;

there is little to know
and all eternity,
O my sister;

there is no hurry,
no haste,
no waste,
only leisure;

infinite leisure
to proclaim
harmony,
our Master.

IX

So haste not,
bright meteor;

waste not strength,
O fair planet,
singing-sister;

move delicate strength,
pause,
never-weary pallor;

gather blue corn-flowers,
bind poppies in your hair,
O Priestess;

teach men
that the sun-disk
is bearable,
and his ardour;

dare further,
stare with me
into the face of Death,
and say,
Love is stronger.

X

Rhodocleia,
rhododendron,
sway, pause, turn again;

rhododendron,
O wide rose,
open, quiver, pause
and close;

rhododendron,
O strong tree,
sway and bend
and speak to me;

utter words
that I may
take
wax
and cut upon my tablets

words to make men pause
and cry
rhododendron
to the sky;

words that men may pause
and kneel,
broken
by this pulse we feel;

rhododendron,
laurel-tree,
sway, pause,
answer me;

you who fled your Lord and Sire,
till he pulsed to such desire
that no woman ever
could

after,
bear his sacred brood;

only singing fools and deft
trees
might speak
his prophecies.

XI

Rhododendron,
O wild-wood,
let no serpent
with drawn hood,
enter,
know the world we know;

rhododendron,
O white snow,
let no mortal ever know
mysteries
within the fold
of purple
and of rose
and gold
cluster
of this sacred tree;

rhododendron,
swear to me,
by his mountain,
by his stream,
none shall mar
the Pythian dream.

XII

We will build an altar here,
swear by wood, by hill, by star,
swear by wind, by curve of bay
where his leaping dolphins lay,

singing to the priests, *on high
build the altar
let life die,
but his song shall never die.*

XIII

Leap as sea-fish
from the water,
toss your arms as fins,
dive under;
where the flute-note
sings of men,
leaving home
and following dream,

bid men follow
as we follow;

as the harp-note tells of steel,
strung to bear immortal peril,
(pleasure such as gods may feel)
bid men feel
as we feel.

The Master

I

He was very beautiful,
the old man,
and I knew wisdom,
I found measureless truth
in his words,
his command
was final;

(how did he understand?)

when I travelled to Miletus
to get wisdom,
I left all else behind,
I fasted,
I worked late,
rose early;
whether I wore simple garments
or intricate
nothing was lost,
each vestment had meaning,
"every gesture is wisdom,"
he taught;
"nothing is lost,"
he said;
I went late to bed
or early,
I caught the dream
and rose dreaming,
and we wrought philosophy on the dream content,
I was content;

nothing was lost
for God is all
and the dream is God;
only to us,

to us
is small wisdom,
but great enough
to know God everywhere;

O he was fair,
even when I flung his words in his teeth,
he said,
"I will soon be dead
I must learn from the young";

his tyranny was absolute,
for I had to love him then,
I had to recognise that he was beyond all-men,
nearer to God
(he was so old)
I had to claim
pardon,
which he granted
with his old head
so wise,
so beautiful
with his mouth so young
and his eyes—

O God,
let there be some surprise in heaven for him,
for no one but you could devise
anything suitable
for him,
so beautiful.

II

I don't know what to suggest,
I can hardly suggest things to God
who with a nod
says, "rise Olympos,
sink into the sea,

O Pelion,
Ossa,
be still'';

I do not know what to say to God,
for the hills
answer his nod,
and the sea
when he tells his daughter,
white Mother
of green
leaves
and green rills
and silver,
to still
tempest
or send peace
and surcease of peril
when a mountain has spit fire:

I did not know how to differentiate
between volcanic desire,
anemones like embers
and purple fire
of violets
like red heat,
and the cold
silver
of her feet:

I had two loves separate;
God who loves all mountains,
alone knew why
and understood
and told the old man
to explain

the impossible,

which he did.

III

What can God give the old man,
who made this possible?

for a woman
breathes fire
and is cold,
a woman sheds snow from ankles
and is warm;
white heat
melts into snow-flake
and violets
turn to pure amethysts,
water-clear:

no,
I did not falter,
I saw the whole miracle,
I knew that the old man made this tenable,
but how could he have foreseen
the impossible?

how could he have known
how each gesture of this dancer
would be hieratic?
words were scrawled on papyrus,
words were written most carefully,
each word was separate
yet each word led to another word,
and the whole made a rhythm
in the air,
till now unguessed at,
unknown.

IV

I was angry at the old man,
I wanted an answer,
a neat answer,

when I argued and said, "well, tell me,
you will soon be dead,
the secret lies with you,"
he said,
"you are a poet";

I do not wish to be treated like a child, a weakling,
so I said,
(I was angry)
"you can not last forever,
the fire of wisdom dies with you,
I have travelled far to Miletus,
you can not stay long now with us,
I came for an answer";

I was angry with the old man
with his talk of the man-strength,
I was angry with his mystery, his mysteries,
I argued till day-break;

O, it was late,
and God will forgive me, my anger,
but I could not accept it.

I could not accept from wisdom
what love taught,
woman is perfect.

V

She is a woman,
yet beyond woman,
yet in woman,
her feet are the delicate pulse of the narcissus bud,
pushing from earth
(ah, where is your man-strength?)
her arms are the waving of the young
male,
tentative,

reaching out
that first evening
alone in a forest;

she is woman,
her thighs are frail yet strong,
she leaps from rock to rock
(it was only a small circle for her dance)

and the hills dance,

she conjures the hills;
"rhododendrons
awake,"
her feet
pulse,
the rhododendrons
wake
there is purple flower
between her marble, her birch-tree white
thighs,
or there is a red flower,

there is a rose flower
parted wide,
as her limbs fling wide in dance
ecstatic
Aphrodite,
there is a frail lavender flower
hidden in grass;

O God, what is it,
this flower
that in itself had power over the whole earth?
for she needs no man,
herself
is that dart and pulse of the male,
hands, feet, thighs,
herself perfect.

VI

Let the old man lie in the earth
(he has troubled men's thought long enough)
let the old man die,
let the old man be of the earth
he is earth,
Father,
O beloved
you are the earth,
he is the earth, Saturn, wisdom,
rock, (O his bones are hard, he is strong, that old man)
let him create a new earth,
and from the rocks of this re-birth
the whole world
must suffer,
only we
who are free,

may foretell,
may prophesy,
he,
(it is he the old man
who will bring a new world to birth)
it is he,
it is he
who already has formed a new earth.

VII

He will trouble the thoughts of men
yet for many an aeon,
they will travel far and wide,
they will discuss all his written words,
his pen will be sacred
they will build a temple
and keep all his sacred writings safe,
and men will come
and men will quarrel
but he will be safe;

they will found temples in his name,
his fame
will be so great
that anyone who has known him
will also be hailed as master,
seer,
interpreter;

only I,
I will escape.

VIII

And it was he himself, he who set me free
to prophesy,

he did not say
"stay,
my disciple,"
he did not say,
"write,
each word I say is sacred,"
he did not say, "teach"
he did not say,
"heal
or seal
documents in my name,"

no,
he was rather casual,
"we won't argue about that"
(he said)
"you are a poet."

IX

So I went forth
blinded a little with the sort of terrible tears
that won't fall;

I said good-bye

and saw his old head
as he turned,
as he left the room
leaving me alone
with all his old trophies,
the marbles, the vases, the stone Sphynx,
the old, old jars from Egypt;
he left me alone with these things
and his old back was bowed;

O God,
those tears didn't come,
how could they?
I went away,
I said,
"I won't have this tyranny
of an old man
he is too old,
I will die,
if I love him;

I can not love him
he is too near
too precious to God."

X

But one does not forget him
who makes all things feasible,
one does not forgive him
who makes God-in-all
possible,
for that is unbearable.

XI

Now can I bear even God,
for a woman's laughter
prophesies
happiness:

(not man, not men,
only one, the old man,
sacred to God);

no man will be present in those mysteries,
yet all men will kneel,
no man will be potent,
important,
yet all men will feel
what it is to be a woman,
will yearn,
burn,
turn from easy pleasure
to hardship
of the spirit,

men will see how long they have been blind,
poor men
poor man-kind
how long
how long
this thought of the man-pulse has tricked them,
has weakened them,
shall see woman,
perfect.

XII

And they did;
I was not the only one that cried
madly,
madly,
we were together,
we were one;

we were together
we were one;
sun-worshippers,

we flung
as one voice
our cry
Rhodocleia;

Rhodocleia,
near to the sun,
we did not say
"pity us,"
we did not say, "look at us,"
we cried,
"O heart of the sun
rhododendron,
Rhodocleia,
we are unworthy your beauty,

you are near beauty the sun,
you are that Lord become woman."

The Poet

I

There were sea-horses and mer-men
and a flat tide-shelf,
there was a sand-dune,
turned moon-ward,
and a trail of wet weed
beyond it,
another of weed,
burnt another colour,
and scattered seed-pods
from the sea-weed;

there was a singing snail,
(does a snail sing?)
a sort of tenuous wail
that was not the wind
nor that one gull,
perched on the half-buried
keel,
nor was it any part of translatable sound,
it might have been, of course,
another sort of reed-bird,
further inland;

inland, there was a pond,
filled with water-lilies;
they opened in fresh-water
but the sea was so near,
one was afraid some inland tide,
some sudden squall,
would sweep up,
sweep in,
over the fresh-water pond,
down the lilies;

that is why I am afraid;
I look at you,
I think of your song,
I see the long trail of your coming,
(your nerves are almost gone)
your song is the wail
of something intangible
that I almost
but not-quite feel.

II

But you are my brother,
it is an odd thing that we meet here;
there is this year
and that year,

my lover,
your lover,
there is death
and the dead past:

but you were not living at all,
and I was half-living,
so where the years blight these others,
we, who were not of the years,
have escaped,
we got nowhere;

they were all going somewhere;

I know you now at this moment, when you turn
and thank me ironically,
(everything you say is ironical)
for the flagon I offer,
(you will have no more white wine);

you are over-temperate in all things;
(is inspiration to be tempered?)
almost, as you pause,
in reply to some extravagance
on my part,
I believe that I have failed,
because I got out of the husk that was my husk,

and was butterfly;

O snail,
I know that you are singing;
your husk is a skull,
your song is an echo,
your song is infinite as the sea,
your song is nothing,
your song is the high-tide that washed away the old
        boat-keel,

the wet weed,
the dry weed,
the seed-pods scattered,
but not you;

you are true
to your self, being true
to the irony
of your shell.

III

Yes,
it is dangerous to get out,
and you shall not fail;
but it is also
dangerous to stay in,
unless one is a snail:

a butterfly has antennae,
is moral
and ironical too.

IV

And your shell is a temple,
I see it at night-fall;
your small coptic temple
is left inland,
in spite of wind,
not yet buried
in sand-storm;

your shell is a temple,
its windows are amber;

you smile
and a candle is set somewhere
on an altar;

everyone has heard of the small coptic temple,
but who knows you,
who dwell there?

V

No,
I don't pretend, in a way, to understand,
nor know you,
nor even see you;

I say,
"I don't grasp his philosophy,
and I don't understand,"

but I put out a hand, touch a cold door,
(we have both come from so far);
I touch something imperishable;
I think,
why should he stay there?
why should he guard a shrine so alone,
so apart,
on a path that leads nowhere?

he is keeping a candle burning in a shrine
where nobody comes,
there must be some mystery
in the air
about him,

he couldn't live alone in the desert,
without vision to comfort him,

there must be voices somewhere.

VI

I am almost afraid to sit on this stone,
a little apart,
(hoping you won't know I am here)

I am almost afraid to look up at the windows,
to watch for that still flame;

I am almost afraid to speak,
certainly won't cry out, "hail,"
or "farewell" or the things people do shout:

I am almost afraid to think to myself,
why,
he is there.

A Dead Priestess Speaks

I

I was not pure,
nor brought
purity to cope
with the world's lost hope,
nor was I insolent;

I went my own way,
quiet and still by day,
advised my neighbour
on the little crop
that faded in the sudden heat,
or brought my seedlings
where hers fell too late
to catch the first
still summer-dew
or late rain-fall of autumn;

I never shone
with glory
among women,
and with men,

I stood apart,
smiling;
they thought me good;

far, far, far
in the wild-wood,
they would have found me other
had they found

me, whom no man yet found,
only the forest-god
of the wet moss,
of the deep underground,
or of the dry rock
parching to the moon:

at noon,
I folded hands; when my hands
lifted up
a moment from the distaff,

I spoke of luck
that got our Arton's son
dictatorship
in a far city;

when I left my room,
it was to tilt a water-jar or fill
a wine-jar with fresh vintage,
not too ripe;

I gave encouragement
and sought,
*do you like this pattern
of the helm
of Jason's boat (a new one)
with the olive?*

I smiled,
I waited,

I was circumspect;

O never, never, never write that I
missed life or loving;

when the loom
of the three spinning Sisters stops,
and she,
the middle spinner, pauses,
while the last
one with the shears,
cuts off the living thread,
then They may read
the pattern
though you may not,

I, being dead.

II

I laughed not overmuch,
nor sang nor cried;
they said, I might have had,
one year,
the prize, the archon offered
for an epitaph
to a dead soldier;

when I left my room
and saw the sunlight
long upon the grass
and knew that day was over,
the night near,

I scratched the tablet-wax
with a small broom
I made of myrtle from the stunted bush
that grows beside our harbour,

for I looked over the sea-wall
to the further sea—
dark, dark and purple;

no one could write, after his *wine-dark sea*,
an epitaph of glory and of spears;

I watched the years go on
like sun on grass,
and shadow across sunlight,

till they said,
O—you remember? trumpets,
the fire, the shout, the glory of the war?

I answered circumspectly,
claiming no
virtue
that helped the wounded
and no fire
that sung of battle ended,

then they said,
ah she is modest, she is purposeful,
and nominated for the Herald's place,
one
Delia of Miletus.

III

I walked sedately at the head of things,
who yet had wings they saw not;
had they seen,
they would have counted me as one of those
old women who were young when I was young,
who wore bright saffron vestments;

I wore white,
as fitting the high-priestess;

ah, at night—
I had my secret thought, my secret way,
I had my secret song,
who sang by day,
the holy metres that the matrons sang,
sung only by those dedicate to life
of civic virtue
and of civic good;

I knew the poor,
I knew the hideous death they die,
when famine lays its bleak hand on the door;
I knew the rich,
sated with merriment,
who yet are sad,
and I was ever glad,
and circumspect
who never knew their life,
nor poor nor rich,
nor entered into strife,
when the new archon spoke of a new war.

IV

Ah, there was fire—
it caught the light
from the wild-olive when it ceased to yield
a proper fruit,
being wild and small and dear
to me at least,
who bit the acrid berries;

I could have eaten ash-leaves
or wild-oak,
I could have grubbed for acorns like a boar,
or like a wild-goat
bitten into bark,

I could have pecked the bay-tree
like a bird,
winter-green berry
or the berried branch
of the wild-oleander;

tasting leaf and root,
I thought at times of poison,
hoped that I
might lie deep in the tangle,
tasting the hemlock
blossom,
and so die;

but I came home,
and the last archon saw
me reach the door, at dawn;

I did not even care what he might say;

he might have said,
Delia of Miletus is a whore,
she wanders in the open street at night;

how is it
I, who do not care, who did not,
was to him as a mother or a bride,
who was but Delia of Miletus
run wild;
he paused, he stood aside;

I waited for the crowd to mutter filth
and stone me from the altar,
but the new archon cried,
fresh honour to Miletus,
to Delia of Miletus who has found
a new brew of bay,

a new liniment of winter-green
and ripe oak-leaf
and berry of wild-olive
that will stay
the after-ravages of the plague
they brought here from Abydos.

V

Honour came to me,
though I sought it not;
I died at mid-day, sleeping;

they did not see the reach of purple-wing
that lifted me out of the little room,
they did not see drift of the purple-fire
that turned the spring-fire
into winter gloom;

they could not see that Spirit
in the day,
that turned the day to ashes,
though the sun
shone straight into the window.

I left the lintel swept,
the wine in jars,
placed
in a row as fitting;
all was neat,
no ash was left upon the hearth,
a few sprays of wild-crocus filled the cup
with the design, copied from one I wove,
once long ago,
of Jason at the helm
with frame of the wild-olive;

they cried aloud,
woe,
woe,
aie,
aie:
they said,
Delia,
Delia,
the high-priestess
here, lies dead.

VI

Would they have given me that simple white
pure slab of untouched marble,
had they known
had my wide wings sprung wide,

how my heart cried,
O, I was never pure nor wise nor good,
I never made a song that told of war,
I was not rich,
I was not very poor,
I stood unsmiling or I smiled
to match
the company about me;

how was it I,
who walked so circumspectly, yet was caught
in the arms of an angry lover,
who said,
late,

late,
I waited too long for you, Delia,
I will devour you,
love you into flame,

O late
my love,
my bride,
Delia of Miletus.

VII

They carved upon the stone
that I was good,
they scattered ashes that were only
ash of bone
and fibre,
burnt by wood,
gathered for ceremonial,
long instituted by the head of kings,
the high-priest from Arcadia;

they spoke of honours,
the line I drew with weaving,
the fine thread,
they told of liniments, I steeped in oil
to heal the burns of those washed here ashore,
when that old ship took light from a pine-torch,
dropped by a drunken sailor:

they told of how I wandered, risking life,
in the cool woods
to cull those herbs,
in this or that
sharp crescent-light;
or the full light
of moon.

EURIPIDES: ION

(Concluding Episode)

XIX

[And last but not least, *deus ex machina* steps forth; intellect, mind, silver but shining with so luminous a splendour that the boy starts back, confusing this emanation of pure-spirit with that other, his spirit-father, her actual brother of Olympos. "Flee not," says Pallas Athené, "you flee no enemy in me," and this most beautiful abstraction of antiquity and of all time, pleads for the great force of the under-mind or the unconscious that so often, on the point of blazing upward into the glory of inspirational creative thought, flares, by a sudden law of compensation, down, making for tragedy, disharmony, disruption, disintegration, but in the end, O, in the end, if we have patience to wait, she says, if we have penetration and faith and the desire actually to follow all those hidden subterranean forces, how great is our reward. "You flee no enemy in me, but one friendly to you," says the shining intellect, standing full armed, in a silver that looks gold in the beams, as we may now picture them, of the actual sun, setting over the crags and pinnacles of Parnassus, shedding its subdued glow upon this group, these warm people who yet remain abstraction; a woman, her son; the haunting memory of a wraith-like priestess; the old, old man; the worldly king and general; the choros, so singularly a unit yet breaking occasionally apart, like dancers, to show individual, human Athenian women of the period, to merge once more into a closed circle of abstract joy or sorrow; the boy again in his manifold guises; the woman who is queen and almost goddess, who now in her joy wishes to be nothing but the mother of Ion; the mother, if she but knew it, of a new culture, of an aesthetic drive and concentrated spiritual force, not to be reckoned with, in terms of any then known values; hardly, even to-day, to be estimated at its true worth. For this new culture was content, as no culture had been before, or has since been, frankly with one and but one supreme quality, perfection. Beyond that, below it and before it, there was nothing. The human mind dehumanized itself, in much the same way (if we may imagine group-consciousness so at work) in which shell-fish may work outward to patterns of exquisite variety and unity. The conscious mind of man had achieved kinship with unconscious forces of most subtle definition. Columns wrought with delicate fluting, whorls of capitals, folds of marble garment, the heel of an athlete or the curls of a god or hero, the head-band of a high-priest or a goddess, the elbow-joint of an archer or the lifted knee of one of the horses of the dioscuri, no matter how dissimilar, had yet one fundamental inner force that framed them, projected them, as (we repeat) a certain genus of deep-sea fish may project its shell. Shell, indeed, left high and dry when the black tide of late Rome and the Middle Ages had drawn far, far out, dragging man and man's aesthetic effort with it. A scattered handful of these creatures or creations is enough to mark, for all time, that high-water mark of human achievement, the welding of strength and delicacy, the valiant yet totally unselfconscious withdrawal of the personality of the artist, who traced on marble, for all time, that thing never to be repeated, faintly to be imitated, at its highest, in the Italian quattrocento, that thing and that thing alone that we mean, when we say, Ionian.

Let not our hearts break before the beauty of Pallas Athené. No; she makes all things possible for us. The human mind to-day pleads for all; nothing is misplaced that in the end may be illuminated by the inner fire of abstract understanding; hate, love, degradation, humiliation, all, all may be examined, given due proportion and dismissed finally, in the light of the mind's vision. To-day, again at a turning-point in the history of the world, the mind stands, to plead, to condone, to explain, to clarify, to illuminate; and, in the name of our magnificent heritage of that Hellenic past, each one of us is responsible to that abstract reality; silver and unattainable yet always present, that spirit again stands holding the balance between the past and the future. What now will we make of it?

And how will we approach it? Not merely through subtle and exquisite preoccupations with shells of its luminous housing; no. Long ago, an olive-tree sprang up. It was sheltered by the Erechtheum. It was worshipped by virgin choros, procession of children, boys and girls; by the older girls; by the wise men of the city; by the heroes about to depart for Marathon; by poet and sculptor, king and visiting prelate. The Persian swept down on the city. We all know of this. We know how not one stone was left upon another, how the old wooden temple that held the ancient dragon and the smiling, ironical, thin and fragile goddess herself, striking it back, fell charred, and buried beneath it, other priceless images, a thin Dioskouros mounting to a horse, a weathered Hermes, a Victory, a stone owl, a plaque, inscribed with legal matter, dating from the days of Solon. The mighty olive-tree had been planted by the very hands of the goddess; it was this gift to men that the gods had placed above the inestimable offering of Poseidon's white, swift horses. The olive was beautiful and useful, it fed and gave that oil, prized alike for food, for anointing Pythian or Isthmian victor, and for ritualistic sacrifice. The charred stump of the tree stood out now among the ruins of the Acropolis. "When our olive-tree dies," the Athenians had been taught from childhood, "our city is lost." Ah lost— lost city!

Tradition has it that one devote scrambled back. He was disobedient to the injunction of his goddess, blatantly for this one time, rebellious. Of nothing, too much. Of one thing too much, and for the last time, that one thing (we may imagine his tense thought, valiant above his broken heart-beats) beauty. Not the beauty of the lyre-note plucked at dawn, not the beauty of ecstasy of the red-wine cup and song among the dancers, not the beauty of the virgin-huntress knee-deep in wild lilies, not the beauty of the cloudy outline (God of men, of gods) your father, O Athené, resting on the hill-tops; not snow, nor cloud, nor thunder, nor wind, nor rain, nor the concrete projected reality of stone coping nor architrave, but the beauty of pure thought—and he would fall here—his ankles burnt with smouldering beams from the little, painted ark-temple; his torn sandals were scorched, his heart beating, his last heart-beat. O yes, he can remember them, his friends in the little, lost city. They are strapping their miserable bundles, trying to fasten overcrowded or almost empty boxes, ready to flee the Persian, the Persian—lost—we can share his thought, feel the vibration of his rebellion, *of nothing too much*—save of this thing. Our love for our lost city.

There was a new war plague that year with a new name, but his lungs and his knees have come this far to defy her injunction (with his last breath) *of nothing too much*. And there by the charred stump of the old, of the immemorial olive, we may hear his last cry. *Of this thing, too much*—

Did he sleep, our rebellious Athenian? What dawn saw him rise? How was he wakened? By cold wind, no doubt, from the sea, that blue sea that, always its traditional enemy, had now deserted Athens for good. Poseidon had won at last. He might easily have sunk the straits in white foam, or better, summoned an earthquake to fling up rock bulwarks against the invading splendour of those purple galleys. The sea did not listen to the propitiatory prayers of the holy denizens of his city. He sent no storm to wreck the enemies of Greece—and yet he, too, was Greek. Faithless and treacherous at the last, he seemed even to encourage with tender sea-breeze the freightage of these robbers. And what had the west to give them that the east had not? Laden with gold and packed with their beaten goblets, the galleys of Xerxes sought wealth here (O, little, ark-like, painted temple of wisdom!) worth all their fabulous trappings, harness for a million stallion, tent-poles of gold, awnings fringed with silver, gold-pricked tapestries. From Athens' ancient enemy, the sea, the dawn came.

Our Athenian's face was black with ashes, so that what

he saw was , no doubt, part of the dishevelled humour of his dreaming. He reached out his frozen hand toward the charred stump of the once sacred olive-tree, to find—

Close to the root of the blackened, ancient stump, a frail silver shoot was clearly discernible, chiselled as it were, against that blackened wood; incredibly frail, incredibly silver, it reached toward the light. Pallas Athené, then, was not dead. Her spirit spoke quietly, a very simple message.

How did·he get back to his people? What did he say when he finally overtook them, perhaps on the old, sacred Eleusinian highway? What was their answer to the rapture of his so simple, so spiritual message, that told his companions of that hope (from which sprang a later Parthenon). Our old tree is not dead. The Persian has not killed it.

To-day? Yesterday? Greek time is like all Greek miracles. Years gain no permanence nor impermanence by a line of curious numbers; numerically 1920, 1922 and again (each time, spring) 1932, we touched the stem of a frail sapling, an olive-tree, growing against the egg-shell marble walls of the Erechtheum.

While one Ionic column stands, stark white and pure on the earth, that name shall live, the power of that goddess shall not have passed, the beauty and the cruelty of her brother shall not be relegated as sheer daemonism or paganism (whatever, God help us, that word has come to mean), while one Ionic column lives to tell of the greatest aesthetic miracle of all-time, welding of beauty and strength, the absolute achievement of physical perfection by the spirit of man, before the world sank into the darkness of late Rome and the Middle Ages, this goddess lives.

> *Flee not,*
> *in me*
> *you flee no enemy,*
> *but one friendly to you,*
> *Pallas.*]

ATHENÉ   Flee not,
             in me
             you flee no enemy,

but one friendly to you,
Pallas;
I come from Athens
in my chariot;
I am sent
by Helios
who fears your reproach;
that is past;

I speak
for Helios;

he is your father;
he gave you to another
so that you might enter
a noble house;
but fearing
(once found out)
that your mother
might slay you,
or you slay your mother,
he sent me;

he would keep this secret;
the Athenians must not know;

but for you,
I fastened my steeds,
to my chariot,
for you,
I came
to reveal
mystery;

Kreousa,
go home;
place your own child
on his
and on your throne.

ION Pallas,
     great daughter of Zeus,
     how could one question
     you?
     how could one doubt
     your speech?
     what was impossible before,
     is clear;
     I am the son
     of Loxias;

KREOUSA now you must listen,
         I speak,
         I praise
         whom I blamed,
         Helios;
         he has repaid
         my loss;
         O, doors,
         O, oracular gates,
         you were black before,
         now
         what light,
         what light
         breaks;
         O, handle,
         I touch you,
         I kiss you,
         O, holy door;

ATHENÉ the gods' pace moves slow,
        do they forget?
        no;
        blessed be the man
        who waits
        (nor doubts)
        for the end
        of the intricate
        plan.

KREOUSA	O, child, come home—
ATHENÉ	lead on, I follow—
ION	what friends, what a road—
KREOUSA	lead to Athens—
ATHENÉ	and a throne—
ION	for me,

ION

CHOROS	Apollo, son of Zeus, son of Leto,
	hail, hail, O, Apollo;
	and you, too, praise the gods, that your heart may be free and your home;
	if you love the gods, you too, shall be loved of fate;
	but you evil doubter, you shall be desolate.

TRILOGY

From The Walls Do Not Fall

To Bryher

for Karnak 1923
from London 1942

[1]

An incident here and there,
and rails gone (for guns)
from your (and my) old town square:

mist and mist-grey, no colour,
still the Luxor bee, chick and hare
pursue unalterable purpose

in green, rose-red, lapis;
they continue to prophesy
from the stone papyrus:

there, as here, ruin opens
the tomb, the temple; enter,
there as here, there are no doors:

the shrine lies open to the sky,
the rain falls, here, there
sand drifts; eternity endures:

ruin everywhere, yet as the fallen roof
leaves the sealed room
open to the air,

so, through our desolation,
thoughts stir, inspiration stalks us
through gloom:

unaware, Spirit announces the Presence;
shivering overtakes us,
as of old, Samuel:

trembling at a known street-corner,
we know not nor are known;
the Pythian pronounces—we pass on

to another cellar, to another sliced wall
where poor utensils show
like rare objects in a museum;

Pompeii has nothing to teach us,
we know crack of volcanic fissure,
slow flow of terrible lava,

pressure on heart, lungs, the brain
about to burst its brittle case
(what the skull can endure!):

over us, Apocryphal fire,
under us, the earth sway, dip of a floor,
slope of a pavement

where men roll, drunk
with a new bewilderment,
sorcery, bedevilment:

the bone-frame was made for
no such shock knit within terror,
yet the skeleton stood up to it:

the flesh? it was melted away,
the heart burnt out, dead ember,
tendons, muscles shattered, outer husk dismembered,

yet the frame held:
we passed the flame: we wonder
what saved us? what for?

[2]

Evil was active in the land,
Good was impoverished and sad;

Ill promised adventure,
Good was smug and fat;

Dev-ill was after us,
tricked up like Jehovah;

Good was the tasteless pod,
stripped from the manna-beans, pulse, lentils:

they were angry when we were so hungry
for the nourishment, God;

they snatched off our amulets,
charms are not, they said, grace;

but gods always face two-ways,
so let us search the old highways

for the true-rune, the right-spell,
recover old values;

nor listen if they shout out,

your beauty, Isis, Aset or Astarte,

is a harlot; you are retrogressive,
zealot, hankering after old flesh-pots;

your heart, moreover,
is a dead canker,

they continue, and
your rhythm is the devil's hymn,

your stylus is dipped in corrosive sublimate,
how can you scratch out

indelible ink of the palimpsest
of past misadventure?

[3]

Let us, however, recover the Sceptre,
the rod of power:

it is crowned with the lily-head
or the lily-bud:

it is Caduceus; among the dying
it bears healing:

or evoking the dead,
it brings life to the living.

[4]

There is a spell, for instance,
in every sea-shell:

continuous, the sea-thrust
is powerless against coral,

bone, stone, marble
hewn from within by that craftsman,

the shell-fish:
oyster, clam, mollusc

is master-mason planning
the stone marvel:

yet that flabby, amorphous hermit
within, like the planet

senses the finite,
it limits its orbit

of being, its house,
temple, fane, shrine:

it unlocks the portals
at stated intervals:

prompted by hunger,
it opens to the tide-flow:

but infinity? no,
of nothing-too-much:

I sense my own limit,
my shell-jaws snap shut

at invasion of the limitless,
ocean-weight; infinite water

can not crack me, egg in egg-shell;
closed in, complete, immortal

full-circle, I know the pull
of the tide, the lull

as well as the moon;
the octopus-darkness

is powerless against
her cold immortality;

so I in my own way know
that the whale

can not digest me:
be firm in your own small, static, limited

orbit and the shark-jaws
of outer circumstance

will spit you forth:
be indigestible, hard, ungiving.

so that, living within,
you beget, self-out-of-self,

selfless,
that pearl-of-great-price.

[6]

In me (the worm) clearly
is no righteousness, but this—

persistence; I escaped spider-snare,
bird-claw, scavenger bird-beak,

clung to grass-blade,
the back of a leaf

when storm-wind
tore it from its stem;

I escaped, I explored

rose-thorn forest,

was rain-swept
down the valley of a leaf;

was deposited on grass,
where mast by jewelled mast

bore separate ravellings
of encrusted gem-stuff

of the mist
from each banner-staff:

unintimidated by multiplicity
of magnified beauty,

such as your gorgon-great
dull eye can not focus

nor compass, I profit
by every calamity;

I eat my way out of it;
gorged on vine-leaf and mulberry,

parasite, I find nourishment:
when you cry in disgust,

a worm on the leaf,
a worm in the dust,

a worm on the ear-of-wheat,
I am yet unrepentant,

for I know how the Lord God
is about to manifest, when I,

the industrious worm,
spin my own shroud.

[7]

Gods, goddesses
wear the winged head-dress

of horns, as the butterfly
antennae,

or the erect king-cobra crest
to show how the worm turns.

[8]

So we reveal our status
with twin-horns, disk, erect serpent,

though these or the double-plume or lotus
are, you now tell us, trivial

intellectual adornment;
poets are useless,

more than that
we, authentic relic,

bearers of the secret wisdom,
living remnant

of the inner band
of the sanctuaries' initiate,

are not only 'non-utilitarian',
we are 'pathetic':

this is the new heresy;
but if you do not even understand what words say,

how can you expect to pass judgement
on what words conceal?

yet the ancient rubrics reveal that
we are back at the beginning:

you have a long way to go,
walk carefully, speak politely

to those who have done their worm-cycle,
for gods have been smashed before

and idols and their secret is stored
in man's very speech,

in the trivial or
the real dream; insignia

in the heron's crest,
the asp's back,

enigmas, rubrics promise as before,
protection for the scribe;

he takes precedence of the priest,
stands second only to the Pharoah.

[9]

Thoth, Hermes, the stylus,
the palette, the pen, the quill endure,

though our books are a floor
of smouldering ash under our feet;

though the burning of the books remains
the most perverse gesture

and the meanest
of man's mean nature,

yet give us, they still cry,
give us books,

folio, manuscript, old parchment
will do for cartridge cases;

irony is bitter truth
wrapped up in a little joke,

and Hatshepsut's name is still circled
with what they call the *cartouche*.

[10]

But we fight for life,
we fight, they say, for breath,

so what good are your scribblings?
this—we take them with us

beyond death; Mercury, Hermes, Thoth
invented the script, letters, palette;

the indicated flute or lyre-notes
on papyrus or parchment

are magic, indelibly stamped
on the atmosphere somewhere,

forever; remember, O Sword,
you are the younger brother, the latter-born,

your Triumph, however exultant,
must one day be over,

*in the beginning
was the Word.*

[16]

Ra, Osiris, *Amen* appeared
in a spacious, bare meeting-house;

he is the world-father,
father of past aeons,

present and future equally;
beardless, not at all like Jehovah,

he was upright, slender,
impressive at the Memnon monolith,

yet he was not out of place
but perfectly at home

in that eighteenth-century
simplicity and grace;

then I woke with a start
of wonder and asked myself,

but whose eyes are those eyes?
for the eyes (in the cold,

I marvel to remember)
were all one texture,

as if without pupil
or all pupil, dark

yet very clear with amber
shining . . .

[21]

Splintered the crystal of identity,
shattered the vessel of integrity,

till the Lord *Amen*,
paw-er of the ground,

bearer of the curled horns,
bellows from the horizon:

here am I, Amen-Ra,
Amen, Aries, the Ram;

time, time for you to begin a new spiral,
see—I toss you into the star-whirlpool;

till pitying, pitying,
snuffing the ground,

here am I, Amen-Ra whispers,
Amen, Aries, the Ram,

be cocoon, smothered in wool,
be Lamb, mothered again.

[22]

Now my right hand,
now my left hand

clutch your curled fleece;
take me home, take me home,

my voice wails from the ground;
take me home, Father:

pale as the worm in the grass,
yet I am a spark

struck by your hoof from a rock:
Amen, you are so warm,

hide me in your fleece,
crop me up with the new-grass;

let your teeth devour me,
let me be warm in your belly,

the sun-disk,
the re-born Sun.

[23]

Take me home
where canals

flow
between iris-banks:

where the heron
has her nest:

where the mantis
prays on the river-reed:

where the grasshopper says
Amen, Amen, Amen.

[39]

We have had too much consecration,
too little affirmation,

too much: but this, this, this
has been proved heretical,

too little: I know, I feel
the meaning that words hide;

they are anagrams, cryptograms,
little boxes, conditioned

to hatch butterflies . . .

[40]

For example:
Osiris equates O-sir-is or O-Sire-is;

Osiris,
the star Sirius,

relates resurrection myth
and resurrection reality

through the ages;
plasterer, crude mason,

not too well equipped, my thought
would cover deplorable gaps

in time, reveal the regrettable chasm,
bridge that before-and-after schism,

(*before Abraham was I am*)
uncover cankerous growths

in present-day philosophy,
in an endeavour to make ready,

as it were, the patient for the Healer;
correlate faith with faith,

recover the secret of Isis,
which is: there was One

in the beginning, Creator,
Fosterer, Begetter, the Same-forever

in the papyrus-swamp
in the Judean meadow.

[43]

*Still the walls do not fall,
I do not know why;*

*there is zrr-hiss,
lightning in a not-known,*

unregistered dimension;

we are powerless,

dust and powder fill our lungs
our bodies blunder

through doors twisted on hinges,
and the lintels slant

cross-wise;
we walk continually

on thin air
that thickens to a blind fog,

then step swiftly aside,
for even the air

is independable,
thick where it should be fine

and tenuous
where wings separate and open,

and the ether
is heavier than the floor,

and the floor sags
like a ship floundering;

we know no rule
of procedure,

we are voyagers, discoverers
of the not-known,

the unrecorded;
we have no map;

possibly we will reach haven,
heaven.

From Tribute to the Angels

To Osbert Sitwell

*. . . possibly we will reach haven,
heaven.*

[1]

Hermes Trismegistus
is patron of alchemists;

his province is thought,
inventive, artful and curious;

his metal is quicksilver,
his clients, orators, thieves and poets;

steal then, O orator,
plunder, O poet,

take what the old-church
found in Mithra's tomb,

candle and script and bell,
take what the new-church spat upon

and broke and shattered;
collect the fragments of the splintered glass

and of your fire and breath,
melt down and integrate,

re-invoke, re-create
opal, onyx, obsidian,

now scattered in the shards
men tread upon.

Your walls do not fall, he said,
because your walls are made of jasper;

but not four-square, I thought,
another shape (octahedron?)

slipped into the place
reserved by rule and rite

for the *twelve foundations,*
for the *transparent glass,*

for *no need of the sun*
nor *moon to shine;*

for the vision as we see
or have seen or imagined it

or in the past invoked
or conjured up or had conjured

by another, was usurped;
I saw the shape

which might have been of jasper,
but it was not four-square.

[3]

I John saw. I testify;
if any man shall add

God shall add unto him the plagues,
but he that sat upon the throne said,

I make all things new.
I John saw. I testify,

but *I make all things new,*
said He of the seven stars,

he of the seventy-times-seven
passionate, bitter wrongs,

He of the seventy-times-seven
bitter, unending wars.

[4]

Not in our time, O Lord,
the plowshare for the sword,

not in our time, the knife,
sated with life-blood and life,

to trim the barren vine;
no grape-leaf for the thorn,

no vine-flower for the crown;
not in our time, O King,

the voice to quell the re-gathering,
thundering storm.

[6]

Never in Rome,
so many martyrs fell;

not in Jerusalem,
never in Thebes,

so many stood and watched
chariot-wheels turning,

saw with their very eyes,
the battle of the Titans,

saw Zeus' thunderbolts in action
and how from giant hands,

the lightning shattered earth
and splintered sky, nor fled

to hide in caves,
but with unbroken will,

with unbowed head, watched
and though unaware, worshipped

and knew not that they worshipped
and that they were

that which they worshipped,
had they known the fire

of strength, endurance, anger
in their hearts,

was part of that same fire
that in a candle on a candle-stick

or in a star,
is known as one of seven,

is named among the seven Angels,
Uriel.

[7]

To Uriel, no shrine, no temple
where the red-death fell,

no image by the city-gate,
no torch to shine across the water,

no new fane in the market-place:
the lane is empty but the levelled wall

is purple as with purple spread
upon an altar,

this is the flowering of the rood,
this is the flowering of the reed,

where, Uriel, we pause to give
thanks that we rise again from death and live.

[8]

Now polish the crucible
and in the bowl distill

a word most bitter, *marah*,
a word bitterer still, *mar*,

sea, brine, breaker, seducer,
giver of life, giver of tears;

now polish the crucible
and set the jet of flame

under, till *marah-mar*
are melted, fuse and join

and change and alter,
mer, mere, mère, mater, Maia, Mary,

Star of the Sea,
Mother.

[16]

Annael—and I remembered the sea-shell
and I remembered the empty lane

and I thought again of people,
daring the blinding rage

of the lightning, and I thought,
there is no shrine, no temple

in the city for that other, *Uriel*,
and I knew his companion,

companion of the fire-to-endure
was another fire, another candle,

was another of seven,
named among the seven Angels,

Annael,
peace of God.

[17]

So we hail them together,
one to contrast the other,

two of the seven Spirits,
set before God

as lamps on the high-altar,
for one must inexorably

take fire from the other
as spring from winter,

and surely never, never
was a spring more bountiful

than this; never, never
was a season more beautiful,

richer in leaf and colour;
tell me, in what other place

will you find the may flowering

153

mulberry and rose-purple?

tell me, in what other city
will you find the may-tree

so delicate, green-white, opalescent
like our jewel in the crucible?

[18]

For Uriel, no temple
but everywhere,

the outer precincts and the squares
are fragrant;

the festival opens as before
with the dove's murmuring;

for Uriel, no temple
but Love's sacred groves,

withered in Thebes and Tyre,
flower elsewhere.

[19]

We see her visible and actual,
beauty incarnate,

as no high-priest of Astoroth
could compel her

.with incense
and potent spell;

we asked for no sign
but she gave a sign unto us;

sealed with the seal of death,
we thought not to entreat her

but prepared us for burial;
then she set a charred tree before us,

burnt and stricken to the heart;
was it may-tree or apple?

[20]

Invisible, indivisible Spirit,
how is it you come so near,

how is it that we dare
approach the high-altar?

we crossed the charred portico,
passed through a frame—doorless—

entered a shrine; like a ghost,
we entered a house through a wall;

then still not knowing
whether (like the wall)

we were there or not-there,
we saw the tree flowering;

it was an ordinary tree
in an old garden-square.

[23]

We are part of it;
we admit the transubstantiation,

not God merely in bread
but God in the other-half of the tree

that looked dead—
did I bow my head?

did I weep? my eyes saw,
it was not a dream

yet it was vision,
it was a sign,

it was *the Angel which redeemed me*,
it was the Holy Ghost—

a half-burnt-out apple-tree
blossoming;

this is the flowering of the rood,
this is the flowering of the wood,

where Annael, we pause to give
thanks that we rise again from death and live.

[24]

Every hour, every moment
has its specific attendant Spirit;

the clock-hand, minute by minute,
ticks round its prescribed orbit;

but this curious mechanical perfection
should not separate but relate rather,

our life, this temporary eclipse
to that other . . .

[25]

. . . of the *no need
of the moon to shine in it,*

for it was ticking minute by minute
(the clock at my bed-head,

with its dim, luminous disc)
when the Lady knocked;

I was talking casually
with friends in the other room,

when we saw the outer hall
grow lighter—then we saw where the door was,

there was no door
(this was a dream, of course),

and she was standing there,
actually, at the turn of the stair.

[29]

We have seen her
the world over,

Our Lady of the Goldfinch,
Our Lady of the Candelabra,

Our Lady of the Pomegranate,
Our Lady of the Chair;

we have seen her, an empress,
magnificent in pomp and grace,

and we have seen her
with a single flower

or a cluster of garden-pinks
in a glass beside her;

we have seen her snood
drawn over her hair,

or her face set in profile
with the blue hood and stars;

we have seen her head bowed down
with the weight of a domed crown,

or we have seen her, a wisp of a girl
trapped in a golden halo;

we have seen her with arrow, with doves
and a heart like a valentine;

we have seen her in fine silks imported
from all over the Levant,

and hung with pearls brought
from the city of Constantine;

we have seen her sleeve
of every imaginable shade

of damask and figured brocade;
it is true,

the painters did very well by her;
it is true, they missed never a line

of the suave turn of the head
or subtle shade of lowered eye-lid

or eye-lids half-raised; you find
her everywhere (or did find),

in cathedral, museum, cloister,
at the turn of the palace stair.

[30]

We see her hand in her lap,

smoothing the apple-green

or the apple-russet silk;
we see her hand at her throat,

fingering a talisman
brought by a crusader from Jerusalem;

we see her hand unknot a Syrian veil
or lay down a Venetian shawl

on a polished table that reflects
half a miniature broken column;

we see her stare past a mirror
through an open window,

where boat follows slow boat on the lagoon;
there are white flowers on the water.

[31]

But none of these, none of these
suggest her as I saw her,

though we approach possibly
something of her cool beneficence

in the gracious friendliness
of the marble sea-maids in Venice,

who climb the altar-stair
at *Santa Maria dei Miracoli,*

or we acclaim her in the name
of another in Vienna,

Maria von dem Schnee,
Our Lady of the Snow.

For I can say truthfully,
her veils were *white as snow,*

*so as no fuller on earth
can white them;* I can say

she looked beautiful, she looked lovely,
she was *clothed with a garment*

down to the foot, but it was not
girt about with a golden girdle,

there was no gold, no colour,
there was no gleam in the stuff

nor shadow of hem and seam,
as it fell to the floor; she bore

none of her usual attributes;
the Child was not with her.

[35]

So she must have been pleased with us,
who did not forgo our heritage

at the grave-edge;
she must have been pleased

with the straggling company of the brush and quill
who did not deny their birthright;

she must have been pleased with us,
for she looked so kindly at us

under her drift of veils,
and she carried a book.

[36]

Ah (you say), this is Holy Wisdom,
Santa Sophia, the SS of the *Sanctus Spiritus,*

so by facile reasoning, logically
the incarnate symbol of the Holy Ghost;

your Holy Ghost was an apple-tree
smouldering—or rather now bourgeoning

with flowers; the fruit of the Tree?
this is the new Eve who comes

clearly to return, to retrieve
what she lost the race,

given over to sin, to death;
she brings the Book of Life, obviously.

[37]

This is a symbol of beauty (you continue),
she is Our Lady universally,

I see her as you project her,
not out of place

flanked by Corinthian capitals,
or in a Coptic nave,

or frozen above the centre door
of a Gothic cathedral;

you have done very well by her
(to repeat your own phrase),

you have carved her tall and unmistakable,
a hieratic figure, the veiled Goddess,

whether of the seven delights,
whether of the seven spear-points.

[38]

O yes—you understand, I say,
this is all most satisfactory,

but she wasn't hieratic, she wasn't frozen,
she wasn't very tall;

she is the Vestal
from the days of Numa,

she carries over the cult
of the *Bona Dea*,

she carries a book but it is not
the tome of the ancient wisdom,

the pages, I imagine, are the blank pages
of the unwritten volume of the new;

all you say, is implicit,
all that and much more;

but she is not shut up in a cave
like a Sibyl; she is not

imprisoned in leaden bars
in a coloured window;

she is Psyche, the butterfly,
out of the cocoon.

[41]

She carried a book, either to imply
she was one of us, with us,

or to suggest she was satisfied
with our purpose, a tribute to the Angels;

yet though the campanili spoke,
Gabriel, Azrael,

though the campɘnili answered,
Raphael, Uriel,

though a distant note over-water
chimed *Annael,* and *Michael*

was implicit from the beginning,
another, deep, un-named, resurging bell

answered, sounding through them all:
remember, where there was

no need of the moon to shine . . .
I saw no temple.

[43]

And the point in the spectrum
where all lights become one,

is white and white is not no-colour,
as we were told as children,

but all-colour;
where the flames mingle

and the wings meet, when we gain
the arc of perfection,

we are satisfied, we are happy,
we begin again;

I John saw. I testify

to rainbow feathers, to the span of heaven

and walls of colour,
the colonnades of jasper;

but when the jewel
melts in the crucible,

we find not ashes, not ash-of-rose,
not a tall vase and a staff of lilies,

not *vas spirituale*,
not *rosa mystica* even,

but a cluster of garden-pinks
or a face like a Christmas-rose.

This is the flowering of the rod,
this is the flowering of the burnt-out wood,

where, Zadkiel, we pause to give
thanks that we rise again from death and live.

London
May 17–31, 1944.

From The Flowering of the Rod

To Norman Holmes Pearson

> *. . . pause to give*
> *thanks that we rise again from death and live.*

[1]

O the beautiful garment,
the beautiful raiment—

do not think of His face
or even His hands,

do not think how we will stand
before Him;

remember the snow
on Hermon;

do not look below
where the blue gentian

reflects geometric pattern
in the ice-floe;

do not be beguiled
by the geometry of perfection

for even now,
the terrible banner

darkens the bridge-head;
we have shown

that we could stand;
we have withstood

the anger, frustration,
bitter fire of destruction;

leave the smouldering cities below
(we have done all we could),

we have given until we have no more to give;
alas, it was pity, rather than love, we gave;

now having given all, let us leave all;
above all, let us leave pity

and mount higher
to love—resurrection.

[2]

I go where I love and where I am loved,
into the snow;

I go to the things I love
with no thought of duty or pity;

I go where I belong, inexorably,
as the rain that has lain long

in the furrow; I have given
or would have given

life to the grain;
but if it will not grow or ripen

with the rain of beauty,
the rain will return to the cloud;

the harvester sharpens his steel on the stone;
but this is not our field,

we have not sown this;

pitiless, pitiless, let us leave

The-place-of-a-skull
to those who have fashioned it.

[3]

In resurrection, there is confusion
if we start to argue; if we stand and stare,

we do not know where to go;
in resurrection, there is simple affirmation,

but do not delay to round up the others,
up and down the street; your going

in a moment like this, is the best proof
that you know the way;

does the first wild-goose stop to explain
to the others? no—he is off;

they follow or not
that is their affair;

does the first wild-goose care
whether the others follow or not?

I don't think so—he is so happy to be off—
he knows where he is going;

so we must be drawn or we must fly,
like the snow-geese of the Arctic circle,

to the Carolinas or to Florida,
or like those migratory flocks

who still (they say) hover
over the lost island, Atlantis;

seeking what we once knew,
we know ultimately we will find

happiness; *to-day shalt thou be
with me in Paradise.*

[4]

Blue-geese, white-geese, you may say,
yes, I know this duality, this double nostalgia;

I know the insatiable longing
in winter, for palm-shadow

and sand and burnt sea-drift;
but in the summer, as I watch

the wave till its edge of foam
touches the hot sand and instantly

vanishes like snow on the equator,
I would cry out, stay, stay;

then I remember delicate enduring frost
and its mid-winter dawn-pattern;

in the hot noon-sun, I think of the grey
opalescent winter-dawn; as the wave

burns on the shingle, I think,
you are less beautiful than frost;

but it is also true that I pray,
O, give me burning blue

and brittle burnt sea-weed
above the tide-line,

as I stand, still unsatisfied,

under the long shadow-on-snow of the pine.

[5]

Satisfied, unsatisfied,
satiated or numb with hunger,

this is the eternal urge,
this is the despair, the desire to equilibrate

the eternal variant;
you understand that insistent calling,

that demand of a given moment,
the will to enjoy, the will to live,

not merely the will to endure,
the will to flight, the will to achievement,

the will to rest after long flight;
but who knows the desperate urge

of those others—actual or perhaps now
mythical birds—who seek but find no rest

till they drop from the highest point of the spiral
or fall from the innermost centre of the ever-narrowing
    circle?

for they remember, they remember, as they sway and
    hover,
what once was—they remember, they remember—

they will not swerve—they have known bliss,
the fruit that satisfies—they have come back—

what if the islands are lost? what if the waters
cover the Hesperides? they would rather remember—

remember the golden apple-trees;

O, do not pity them, as you watch them drop one by
    one,

for they fall exhausted, numb, blind
but in certain ecstasy,

for theirs is the hunger
for Paradise.

[6]

So I would rather drown, remembering—
than bask on tropic atolls

in the coral-seas; I would rather drown,
remembering—than rest on pine or fir-branch

where great stars pour down
their generating strength, Arcturus

or the sapphires of the Northern Crown;
I would rather beat in the wind, crying to these others:

yours is the more foolish circling,
yours is the senseless wheeling

round and round—yours has no reason—
I am seeking heaven;

yours has no vision,
I see what is beneath me, what is above me,

what men say is-not—I remember,
I remember, I remember—you have forgot:

you think, even before it is half-over,
that your cycle is at an end,

but you repeat your foolish circling—again, again,
    again;

again, the steel sharpened on the stone;

again, the pyramid of skulls;
I gave pity to the dead,

O blasphemy, pity is a stone for bread,
only love is holy and love's ecstasy

that turns and turns and turns about one centre,
reckless, regardless, blind to reality,

that knows the Islands of the Blest are there,
for *many waters can not quench love's fire.*

[7]

Yet resurrection is a sense of direction,
resurrection is a bee-line,

straight to the horde and plunder,
the treasure, the store-room,

the honeycomb;
resurrection is remuneration,

food, shelter, fragrance
of myrrh and balm.

[8]

I am so happy,
I am the first or the last

of a flock or a swarm;
I am *full of new wine*;

I am branded with a word,
I am burnt with wood,

drawn from glowing ember,

not cut, not marked with steel;

I am the first or the last to renounce
iron, steel, metal;

I have gone forward,
I have gone backward,

I have gone onward from bronze and iron,
into the Golden Age.

[9]

No poetic phantasy
but a biological reality,

a fact: I am an entity
like bird, insect, plant

or sea-plant cell;
I live; I am alive;

take care, do not know me,
deny me, do not recognise me,

shun me; for this reality
is infectious—ecstasy.

[10]

It is no madness to say
you will fall, you great cities,

(now the cities lie broken);
it is not tragedy, prophecy

from a frozen Priestess,
a lonely Pythoness

who chants, who sings
in broken hexameters,

doom, doom to city-gates,
to rulers, to kingdoms;

it is simple reckoning, algebraic,
it is geometry on the wing,

not patterned, a gentian
in an ice-mirror,

yet it is, if you like, a lily
folded like a pyramid,

a flower-cone,
not a heap of skulls;

it is a lily, if you will,
each petal, a kingdom, an aeon,

and it is the seed of a lily
that having flowered,

will flower again;
it is that smallest grain,

the least of all seeds
that grows branches

where the birds rest;
it is that flowering balm,

it is heal-all,
everlasting;

it is the greatest among herbs
and becometh a tree.

HELEN IN EGYPT

Pallinode

Book One

[1]

*We all know the story of Helen of Troy but few of us have
followed her to Egypt. How did she get there? Stesichorus of
Sicily in his Pallinode, was the first to tell us. Some centu-
ries later, Euripides repeats the story. Stesichorus was said
to have been struck blind because of his invective against
Helen, but later was restored to sight, when he reinstated
her in his Pallinode. Euripides, notably in The Trojan
Women, reviles her, but he also is "restored to sight." The
later, little understood Helen in Egypt, is again a Pallinode,
a defence, explanation or apology.*

*According to the Pallinode, Helen was never in Troy. She
had been transposed or translated from Greece into Egypt.
Helen of Troy was a phantom, substituted for the real
Helen, by jealous deities. The Greeks and the Trojans alike
fought for an illusion.*

> Do not despair, the hosts
> surging beneath the Walls,
> (no more than I) are ghosts;
>
> do not bewail the Fall,
> the scene is empty and I am alone,
> yet in this Amen-temple,

I hear their voices,
there is no veil between us,
only space and leisure

and long corridors of lotus-bud
furled on the pillars,
and the lotus-flower unfurled,

with reed of the papyrus
Amen (or Zeus we call him)
brought me here;

fear nothing of the future or the past,
He, God, will guide you,
bring you to this place,

as he brought me, his daughter,
twin-sister of twin-brothers
and Clytaemnestra, shadow of us all;

the old enchantment holds,
here there is peace
for Helena, Helen hated of all Greece.

[2]

*Lethe, as we all know, is the river of forgetfulness for the
shadows, passing from life to death. But Helen, myste-
riously transposed to Egypt, does not want to forget. She is
both phantom and reality.*

The potion is not poison,
it is not Lethe and forgetfulness
but everlasting memory,

the glory and the beauty of the ships,
the wave that bore them onward
and the shock of hidden shoal,

the peril of the rocks,

the weary fall of sail,
the rope drawn taut,

the breathing and breath-taking
climb and fall, mountain and valley
challenging, the coast

drawn near, drawn far,
the helmsman's bitter oath
to see the goal receding

in the night; everlasting, everlasting
nothingness and lethargy of waiting;
O Helen, Helen, Daemon that thou art,

we will be done forever
with this charm, this evil philtre,
this curse of Aphrodite;

so they fought, forgetting women,
hero to hero, sworn brother and lover,
and cursing Helen through eternity.

[3]

Her concern is with the past, with the anathema or curse.
But to the Greeks who perished on the long voyage out, or
who died imprecating her, beneath the Walls, she says,
"you are forgiven." They did not understand what she
herself can only dimly apprehend. She may perceive the
truth, but how explain it? Is it possible that it all happened,
the ruin—it would seem not only of Troy, but of the "holo-
caust of the Greeks," of which she speaks later—in order
that two souls or two soul-mates should meet? It almost
seems so.

Alas, my brothers,
Helen did not walk
upon the ramparts,

she whom you cursed
was but the phantom and the shadow thrown
of a reflection;

you are forgiven for I know my own,
and God for his own purpose
wills it so, that I

stricken, forsaken draw to me,
through magic greater than the trial of arms,
your own invincible, unchallenged Sire,

Lord of your legions, King of Myrmidons,
unconquerable, a mountain and a grave,
Achilles;

few were the words we said,
nor knew each other,
nor asked, are you Spirit?

are you sister? are you brother?
are you alive?
are you dead?

the harpers will sing forever
of how Achilles met Helen
among the shades,

but we were not, we are not shadows;
as we walk, heel and sole
leave our sandal-prints in the sand,

though the wounded heel treads lightly
and more lightly follow,
the purple sandals.

[4]

Had they met before? Perhaps. Achilles was one of the

princely suitors for her hand, at the court of her earthly
father, Tyndareus of Sparta. But this Helen is not to be
recognized by earthly splendour nor this Achilles by accou-
trements of valour. It is the lost legions that have conditi-
oned their encounter, and "the sea-enchantment in his
eyes."

How did we know each other?
was it the sea-enchantment in his eyes
of Thetis, his sea-mother?

what was the token given?
I was alone, bereft,
and wore no zone, no crown,

and he was shipwrecked,
drifting without chart,
famished and tempest-driven

the fury of the tempest in his eyes,
the bane of battle
and the legions lost;

for that was victory
and Troy-gates broken
in memory of the Body,

wounded, stricken,
the insult of the charioteer,
the chariot furiously driven,

the Furies' taunt?
take heart Achilles, for you may not die,
immortal and invincible;

though the Achilles-heel treads lightly,
still I feel the tightening muscles,
the taut sinews quiver,

as if I, Helen, had withdrawn

from the bruised and swollen flesh,
the arrow from its wound.

This was the token, his mortality;
immortality and victory
were dissolved;

I am no more immortal,
I am man among the millions,
no hero-god among the Myrmidons;

some said a bowman from the Walls
let fly the dart, some said it was Apollo,
but I, Helena, know it was Love's arrow;

the body honoured
by the Grecian host
was but an iron casement,

it was God's plan
to melt the icy fortress of the soul,
and free the man;

God's plan is other than the priests disclose;
I did not know why
(in dream or in trance)

God had summoned me hither,
until I saw the dim outline
grown clearer,

as the new Mortal,
shedding his glory,
limped slowly across the sand.

[6]

How did we greet each other?

here in this Amen-temple,
I have all-time to remember;

he comes, he goes;
I do not know that memory calls him,
or what Spirit-master

summons him to release
(as God released him)
the imprisoned, the lost;

few were the words we said,
but the words are graven on stone,
minted on gold, stamped upon lead;

they are coins of a treasure
or the graded weights
of barter and measure;

"I am a woman of pleasure,"
I spoke ironically into the night,
for he had built me a fire,

he, Achilles, piling brushwood,
finding an old flint in his pouch,
"I thought I had lost that";

few were the words we said,
"I am shipwrecked, I am lost,"
turning to view the stars,

swaying as before the mast,
"the season is different,
we are far from—from—"

let him forget,
Amen, All-father,
let him forget.

[7]

Helen achieves the difficult task of translating a symbol in time, into timeless-time or hieroglyph or ancient Egyptian time. She knows the script, she says, but we judge that this is intuitive or emotional knowledge, rather than intellectual. In any case, a night-bird swooped toward them, in their first encounter on the beach. To Achilles, lately arrived from Troy and the carnage of battle, this is a "carrion creature," but Helen would banish these memories. She says she is "instructed," she is enchanted, rather. For from the depth of her racial inheritance, she invokes (as the perceptive visitor to Egypt must always do) the symbol or the "letter" that represents or recalls the protective mother-goddess. This is no death-symbol but a life-symbol, it is Isis or her Greek counterpart, Thetis, the mother of Achilles.

We huddled over the fire,
was there ever such a brazier?
a night-bird hooted past,

he started, "a curious flight,
a carrion creature—what—"
(dear God, let him forget);

I said, "there is mystery in this place,
I am instructed, I know the script,
the shape of this bird is a letter,

they call it the hieroglyph;
strive not, it is dedicate
to the goddess here, she is Isis";

"Isis," he said, "or Thetis," I said,
recalling, remembering, invoking
his sea-mother;

flame, I prayed, *flame forget,
forgive and forget the other,*

let my heart be filled with peace,

let me love him, as Thetis, his mother,
for I knew him, I saw in his eyes
the sea-enchantment, but he

knew not yet, Helen of Sparta,
knew not Helen of Troy,
knew not Helena, hated of Greece.

[8]

How could I hide my eyes?
how could I veil my face?
with ash or charcoal from the embers?

I drew out a blackened stick,
but he snatched it,
he flung it back,

"what sort of enchantment is this?
what art will you wield with a fagot?
are you Hecate? are you a witch?

a vulture, a hieroglyph,
the sign or the name of a goddess?
what sort of goddess is this?

where are we? who are you?
where is this desolate coast?
who am I? am I a ghost?"

"you are living, O child of Thetis,
as you never lived before,"
then he caught at my wrist,

"Helena, cursed of Greece,
I have seen you upon the ramparts,
no art is beneath your power,

you stole the chosen, the flower
of all-time, of all-history,
my children, my legions;

for you were the ships burnt,
O cursèd, O envious Isis,
you—you—a vulture, a hieroglyph";

"Zeus be my witness," I said,
"it was he, Amen dreamed of all this
phantasmagoria of Troy,

it was dream and a phantasy";
O Thetis, O sea-mother,
I prayed, as he clutched my throat

with his fingers' remorseless steel,
let me go out, let me forget,
let me be lost . . . .

O Thetis, O sea-mother, I prayed under his cloak,
let me remember, let me remember,
forever, this Star in the night.

Book Two

[1]

But Helen seems concerned not only with the mystery of
their reconciliation but with the problem of why he had, in
the first instance, attacked her. There seems this latent hos-
tility; with her love, there is fear, yet there is strength, too,
and defiance not only of Achilles, but of the whole powerful
war-faction.

Perhaps he was right
to call me Hecate and a witch;
I do not care for separate

might and grandeur,
I do not want to hear of Agamemnon
and the Trojan Walls,

I do not want to recall
shield, helmet, greaves,
though he wore them,

for that, I might recall them,
being part of his first
unforgettable anger;

I do not want to forget his anger,
not only because it brought Helen
to sleep in his arms,

but because he was, in any case,
defeated; if he strangled her
and flung her to the vultures,

still, he had lost
and they had lost—
the war-Lords of Greece.

[2]

It is the burning ember
that I remember,
heart of the fire,

consuming the Greek heroes;
it is the funeral pyre;
it is incense from the incense-trees,

wafted here through the columns;
never, never do I forget the host,
the chosen, the flower

of all-time, of all-history;

it was they who struck,
as the flint, the spark

of his anger, "no art is beneath your power";
what power drew them to me?
a hieroglyph, repeated endlessly,

upon the walls, the pillars,
the thousand-petalled lily;
they are not many, but one,

enfolded in sleep,
as the furled lotus-bud,
or with great wings unfurled,

sailing in ecstasy,
the western sea,
climbing sea-mountains,

dividing the deep valleys of the sea;
but now, go, go,
Achilles from me;

I feel the lure of the invisible,
I am happier here alone
in this great temple,

with this great temple's
indecipherable hieroglyph;
I have "read" the lily,

I can not "read" the hare, the chick, the bee,
I would study and decipher
the indecipherable Amen-script.

[3]

We were right. Helen herself denies an actual intellectual
knowledge of the temple-symbols. But she is nearer to them

than the instructed scribe; for her, the secret of the stone-
writing is repeated in natural or human symbols. She her-
self is the writing.

> I said, I was instructed in the writ;
> but I had only heard of it,
> when our priests decried
>
> papyrus fragments,
> travellers brought back,
> as crude, primeval lettering;
>
> I had only seen a tattered scroll's
> dark tracing of a caravel
> with a great sun's outline,
>
> but inked-in, as with shadow;
> it seemed a shadow-sun,
> the boat, a picture of a toy;
>
> I was not interested,
> I was not instructed,
> nor guessed the inner sense of the hieratic,
>
> but when the bird swooped past,
> that first evening,
> I seemed to know the writing,
>
> as if God made the picture
> and matched it
> with a living hieroglyph;
>
> how did I know the vulture?
> why did I invoke the mother?
> why was he seized with terror?
>
> in the dark, I must have looked
> an inked-in shadow; but with his anger,
> that ember, I became

what his accusation made me,
Isis, forever with that Child,
the Hawk Horus.

[4]

Helen is a Greek, a Spartan, born from a sea-faring peo-
ple. Although in Egypt, it is not the primitive caravel, as
she calls the shadow or death-ship of Osiris, that she visual-
izes, when she would recall the host of Spirits. Her vision is
wholly Greek, though she returns to the sacred Egyptian
lily for her final inspiration.

This is the spread of wings,
whether the Straits claimed them
or the Cyclades,

whether they floundered on the Pontic seas
or ran aground before the Hellespont,
whether they shouted Victory at the gate,

whether the bowmen shot them from the Walls,
whether they crowded surging through the breach,
or died of fever on the smitten plain,

whether they rallied and came home again,
in the worn hulks, half-rotted from the salt
or sun-warped on the beach,

whether they scattered or in companies,
or three or two sought the old ways of home,
whether they wandered as Odysseus did,

encountering new adventure, they are one;
no, I was not instructed, but I "read" the script,
I read the writing when he seized my throat,

this was his anger,
they were mine, not his,

the unnumbered host;

mine, all the ships,
mine, all the thousand petals of the rose,
mine, all the lily-petals,

mine, the great spread of wings,
the thousand sails,
the thousand feathered darts

that sped them home,
mine, the one dart in the Achilles-heel,
the thousand-and-one, mine.

HERMETIC DEFINITION

Winter Love

(*Espérance*)
(January 3-April 15, 1959)

[2]

If I thought of you, I only thought
of something that endured, that might endure;
I did not know of Circe and her power,

I had not even heard Calypso named, nor Nausicaä,
Penelope was a far-off dream of home,
and others and the quarrel in the tents

(fight for Criseus, war for Briseus)
was only a local matter, far below
the turrets and the ramparts and the Wall;

I loved Achilles finally, in *Leukè*,
but I let him go, back to the sea,
back to his mother, Thetis;

so he was absorbed, re-claimed by his own element?
I do not know, Odysseus—your name is unfamiliar;
I had not thought of it nor spoken it,

for ten years—it is more than ten years;
then, you were in and out as they all were at the Palace,
it is more, more than ten years . . .

So we were together
though I did not think of you
for ten years;

it is more than ten years
and the long time after;
I was with you in Calypso's cave?

no, no—I had never heard of her,
but I remember the curve of honey-flower
on an old wall, I recall

the honey-flower as I saw it
or seemed to see it
for the first time,

its horn was longer, whiter—
what do I mean?
"bite clear the stem

and suck the honey out,"
a child companion or old grandam
taught me to suck honey

from the honey-flower;
what is Calypso's cave?
that is your grotto, your adventure;

how could I love again, ever?
repetition, repetition, Achilles, Paris, Menelaus?
but you are right, you are right,

there is something left over,
the first unsatisfied desire—
the first time, that first kiss,

the rough stones of a wall,

the fragrance of honey-flowers, the bees,
and how I would have fallen but for a voice,

calling through the brambles
and tangle of bay-berry
and rough broom,

Helen, Helen, come home;
there was a Helen before there was a War,
but who remembers her?

[6]

The-tis—Sea-'tis, I played games like this;
I had long reveries, invoked the future,
re-invoked the past, syllables, mysteries, numbers;

I must have turned a secret key, unwittingly,
when I said Odysseus—when did I say Odysseus?
how did I call you back, or how did I come back?

memory has its own strange Circe-magic,
and forgetting, stranger; forgetting utterly, I dropped
a screen, a shutter; a heavy door clanged

between Helen-Helen; "they have gone,"
"where have they gone?" "down to the Sea,
to send Odysseus off—" *"Odysseus—"*

"he was only waiting for his Ship,
a special Ship, ancestral,
the prow is painted with the ancient Eyes."

I was to meet you, I was to meet you
under the oleanders,
I was to meet you again;

"a special Ship, for festival," they said,
so Helen stared, a Maiden, still a Maiden,

though last night, escaped the grandam,

Helen was conceived under the oleanders,
that is, Helen, the future Helen
that wrecked citadels, was born.

[16]

O, do not bring snow-water
but fresh snow;
I would be bathed with stars,

new fallen from heaven,
one with the cloud,
my forehead ringed

with icy frost, a crown;
let my mind flash with blades,
let thought return,

unravel the thick skein,
woven of tangled memory and desire,
lust of the body, hunger, cold and thirst;

our hidden lair has sanctified *Virgo*,
the lost, unsatisfied, the broken tryst,
the half-attained;

love built on dreams
of the forgotten first unsatisfied embrace,
is satisfied.

[19]

Strophe

Odysseus' fretful brow,
Achilles' cunning steel,
and Paris' apple—you have them now,

the adventure and the glory
and the seeds of fruit to sow—
how many grains of pomegranate or apple?

conjure a magic circle of fruit-trees,
with roots to hold *Leuké*, the island-Helen,
in a firm embrace,

an inescapable net,
until the flowers are full
and waft and spill fragrance, enchantment;

who can break the will
of seed to grow?
Paris-Oenone?

Helen, commend their happiness
and so invoke the greater bliss
of Helios-Helen-Eros.

[20]

ANTISTROPHE

Rise from your apathy, your dream,
the die was cast and Helen lost;
leave lovers to their happiness

and grope your way, ignoble and defenceless
in the dark; yours was the guilt;
slough off the fantasy, accept the tangible,

go out, go out, go forth,
renounce the cult of dream for stark reality,
the ashes, the dark scarf,

the veils of widowhood;
you are bereft,
accept the accomplished fact;

beyond, beyond, beyond,
when your bare feet
bleed with the salty wrack

of a strange coast,
and your hair hangs,
loosed from its golden snood,

in snaky tangles, lift a stone
and taste the salt of earth, the salt of sea,
and with the stone, strike at your breast and cry,

"alas, alas, mine was the blame,
mine was the guilt";
down, down, down the path of glory,

the Sun goes into the dark,
the Gods decree
that Helen is deserted utterly.

[21]

O ebony island, O tall cypress-trees,
now I am blessed anew as my dark veils
cling close and close and make an image of me,

a cypress-Helen, *vierge* and widow, the *femme noire*;
now I am wrapped about
with myrrh and incense,

Egypt's balm and savour
of the burnt Phoenix-nest,
l'île blanche is *l'île noire*;

tighten my bounds,
O unseen and unknown,
wrap me round and round

with Egypt's linen as the dead are wrapped,
mystically cut, cauterise

as with fire, the wound from which

the heart and entrails were drawn out;
a shell? a shattered heart?
no heart is left to heal.

[24]

Helios-Helen-Eros? Is that Menelaus?
is that the golden first love, innocence?
is that the Child before the Child was born,

imagined with the cap-crown of bright hair,
inheritance of the "golden Menelaus"?
not Menelaus, but myself gazed up at me,

in the veiled glance of Helen-Hermione;
they said there was a Child in *Leuké*,
they said it was the Child, Euphorion,

Achilles' Child, grandam,
or fantasy of Paris and a Child
or a wild moment that begot a Child,

when long ago, the *Virgo* breasts swelled
under the savage kiss of ravening Odysseus;
yes, yes, grandam, but actually and in reality,

small fists unclosed, small hands fondled me,
and in the inmost dark,
small feet searched foot-hold;

Hermione lived her life and lives in history;
Euphorion, *Espérance*, the infinite bliss,
lives in the hope of something that will be,

the past made perfect;
this is the tangible
this is reality.

[25]

The golden apples of the Hesperides,
the brushed-bloom of the pollen
on the wing of ravishing butterfly or plundering bee;

the gold of evanescence or the gold
of heavy-weighted treasure,
which will out-weigh the other?

grandam, great *Grande Dame*,
we will go on together,
and find the way to hyacinths by a river,

where a harp-note sounded
and a moment later—
grandam, great *Grande Dame*, He is here with us,

in notes ascending and descending from his lyre,
your Child, my Child and Helios' Child, no other,
to lure us on, on, on, Euphorion, *Espérance*.

[27]

Grandam, midwife, *Sage-Femme*,
let me rest, let me rest,
I can't struggle any more;

far, far, let them beget their children
in the wastes or palaces; what is their happiness,
their bliss to this accomplishment?

Oenone, O, Oenone,
live your life, I need no longer chafe
in fantasy or remembrance or regret;

grandam, midwife, *Sage-Femme*,
I pray you, as with his last breath,
a man might pray, keep *Espérance*,

our darling from my sight,
for bliss so great,
the thought of that soft touch,

would drag me back to life
and I would rest;
grandam, great *Grande Dame*,

midwife and *Sage-Femme*,
you brought Him forth in darkness,
while I slept.

[28]

I am delirious now and mean to be,
the whole earth shudders with my ecstasy,
take *Espérance* away;

cruel, cruel *Sage-Femme*,
to place him in my arms,
cruel, cruel *Grande Dame*,

to pull my tunic down,
so Odysseus sought my breast
with savage kiss;

cruel, cruel midwife,
so secretly to steal my phantom self,
my invisibility, my hopelessness, my fate,

the guilt, the blame, the desolation,
Paris slain to rise again
and find Oenone and mortality,

Achilles' flight to Thetis
and the Sea (deserting *Leuké*),
Menelaus with his trophies in the palace,

Odysseus—take the Child away,

cruel, cruel is Hope,
terrible the weight of honey and of milk,

cruel, cruel, the thought of Love,
while Helen's breasts swell, painful
with the ambrosial sap, *Amrita*

that must be given;
I die in agony whether I give or do not give;
cruel, cruel *Sage-Femme*,

wiser than all the regents of God's throne,
why do you torture me?
come, come, O *Espérance*,

Espérance, O golden bee,
take life afresh and if you must,
so slay me.